LIQUEUR

Edible

Series Editor: Andrew F. Smith

EDIBLE is a revolutionary series of books dedicated to food and drink
that explores the rich history of cuisine. Each book reveals the global
history and culture of one type of food or beverage.

Already published

Apple Erika Janik, *Avocado* Jeff Miller, *Banana* Lorna Piatti-Farnell, *Barbecue*
Jonathan Deutsch and Megan J. Elias, *Beans* Nathalie Rachel Morris, *Beef* Lorna
Piatti-Farnell, *Beer* Gavin D. Smith, *Berries* Heather Arndt Anderson, *Biscuits
and Cookies* Anastasia Edwards, *Brandy* Becky Sue Epstein, *Bread* William Rubel,
Breakfast Cereal Kathryn Cornell Dolan, *Cabbage* Meg Muckenhoupt,
Cake Nicola Humble, *Caviar* Nichola Fletcher, *Champagne* Becky Sue Epstein,
Cheese Andrew Dalby, *Chillies* Heather Arndt Anderson, *Chocolate* Sarah Moss
and Alexander Badenoch, *Cocktails* Joseph M. Carlin, *Coconut* Constance L.
Kirker and Mary Newman, *Cod* Elisabeth Townsend, *Coffee* Jonathan Morris,
Corn Michael Owen Jones, *Curry* Colleen Taylor Sen, *Dates* Nawal Nasrallah,
Doughnut Heather Delancey Hunwick, *Dumplings* Barbara Gallani, *Edible
Flowers* Constance L. Kirker and Mary Newman, *Edible Insects* Gina Louise
Hunter, *Eggs* Diane Toops, *Fats* Michelle Phillipov, *Figs* David C. Sutton, *Foie
Gras* Norman Kolpas, *Game* Paula Young Lee, *Gin* Lesley Jacobs Solmonson,
Hamburger Andrew F. Smith, *Herbs* Gary Allen, *Herring* Kathy Hunt, *Honey* Lucy
M. Long, *Hot Dog* Bruce Kraig, *Hummus* Harriet Nussbaum, *Ice Cream* Laura
B. Weiss, *Jam, Jelly and Marmalade* Sarah B. Hood, *Lamb* Brian Yarvin,
Lemon Toby Sonneman, *Liqueur* Lesley Jacobs Solmonson, *Lobster* Elisabeth
Townsend, *Melon* Sylvia Lovegren, *Milk* Hannah Velten, *Moonshine* Kevin R.
Kosar, *Mushroom* Cynthia D. Bertelsen, *Mustard* Demet Güzey, *Nuts* Ken
Albala, *Offal* Nina Edwards, *Olive* Fabrizia Lanza, *Onions and Garlic* Martha
Jay, *Oranges* Clarissa Hyman, *Oyster* Carolyn Tillie, *Pancake* Ken Albala, *Pasta
and Noodles* Kantha Shelke, *Pickles* Jan Davison, *Pie* Janet Clarkson, *Pineapple*
Kaori O'Connor, *Pizza* Carol Helstosky, *Pomegranate* Damien Stone, *Pork*
Katharine M. Rogers, *Potato* Andrew F. Smith, *Pudding* Jeri Quinzio, *Rice* Renee
Marton, *Rum* Richard Foss, *Saffron* Ramin Ganeshram, *Salad* Judith Weinraub,
Salmon Nicolaas Mink, *Sandwich* Bee Wilson, *Sauces* Maryann Tebben,
Sausage Gary Allen, *Seaweed* Kaori O'Connor, *Shrimp* Yvette Florio Lane,
Soda and Fizzy Drinks Judith Levin, *Soup* Janet Clarkson, *Spices* Fred Czarra,
Sugar Andrew F. Smith, *Sweets and Candy* Laura Mason, *Tea* Helen Saberi,
Tequila Ian Williams, *Tomato* Clarissa Hyman, *Truffle* Zachary Nowak,
Vanilla Rosa Abreu-Runkel, *Vodka* Patricia Herlihy, *Water* Ian Miller, *Whiskey*
Kevin R. Kosar, *Wine* Marc Millon, *Yoghurt* June Hersh

Liqueur

A Global History

Lesley Jacobs Solmonson

REAKTION BOOKS

To DS and RS
The most important 'ingredients' in my life

Published by Reaktion Books Ltd
Unit 32, Waterside
44–48 Wharf Road
London N1 7UX, UK
www.reaktionbooks.co.uk

First published 2024
Copyright © Lesley Jacobs Solmonson 2024

Printed and bound in India by Replika Press Pvt. Ltd

A catalogue record for this book is available from the British Library

ISBN 978 1 78914 853 4

Contents

Introduction

In *Nouvelle chymie du goût et de l'odorat* (New Chemistry of Taste and Smell; 1774), author Polycarpe Poncelet wrote, 'I look on a well-prepared liqueur as a species of musical air.' He posited that, just as a well-chosen group of notes can produce a pleasant harmony, so too can a liqueur when the proper balance of flavours is employed. Poncelet's 'musical air' is an eloquent, and poetic, observation about the power that liqueur can possess. Indeed, this sweetened spirit has played many influential roles throughout history. Sometimes it is akin to a soloist in an orchestra, controlling the melody. At other times, it is just a background note. But, regardless of its changing role, it is always there.

The story of liqueur is a compelling tale of alchemy and empires, exploration and industrialization, medicine and recreation, royalty and the common man. Before people imbibed sweet spirits, they had enjoyed fermented, honeyed beverages, which have been documented as early as circa 7000 BCE in China. Crude distillation possibly dates to the fifth century BCE, but the process of actually distilling spirits did not arrive in any sophisticated form until the ninth century. The Islamic alchemist Jābir ibn Ḥayyān, known in the West as Geber, invented the first alembic still. This consisted of two vessels connected by a

Elixir d'Anvers, a herbal, digestive liqueur created in 1863 by the Belgian medical student François-Xavier de Beukelaer.

tube: one held a fermented beverage, in this case wine, the other was empty. When the wine was heated, it separated the alcohol from the water, creating a vapour that travelled through the tube and condensed in the other container. The condensation then returned to its liquid state, which was now pure alcohol. This transformation made possible the conversion of a lower alcohol-by-volume (ABV) beverage into a higher ABV 'spirit'. The alchemists called it *al-kohl*, from which we get our word 'alcohol', and they quickly realized that these strong spirits – when augmented by healthful herbs, roots and spices – made effective medicines.

When the process of distillation reached Europe (the Italian peninsula, to be exact) around the eleventh century, monks and physicians applied it to the production of healing tonics. There was only one problem, and it was a huge one. These elixirs – created from various bitter botanicals like artemisia, gentian and cinchona – had an immensely unpleasant taste. And so, the Mary Poppins-esque question had to be asked: just how to make the medicine go down?

EXTRAIT DE VIANDE DE LA Cᴵᴱ LIEBIG
CHIMISTES CELEBRES.
1) Geber avec son maître Giafar el Ssâdik (8ᵉ siècle).

Liebig Meat Company trade card in the series 'Famous Chemists' showcases Geber, 1903.

Bottle of crème
de cacao, c. 1950s.

The answer arrived along with Western European soldiers returning from the Crusades in the Holy Land. These men brought sugar cane home with them. At first, the refined version of the cane was a luxury only for the wealthy. However, as sugar production became more advanced and widespread, sugar became a more accessible commodity, eventually replacing honey as the sweetener of choice. While the history is hazy, it is thought that the medieval alchemist Arnaldus de Villanova (*c.* 1240–1311) created the first true liqueur, most likely based on brandy spirit sweetened with sugar. Villanova dubbed these treatments 'cordials', after the Latin term *cordialis* (of or pertaining to the heart). Not only did these medicinal cordials taste better than their harsh forefathers, they had the added benefit of making the patient feel pretty darn good.

While Villanova used grape-based brandy for his cordials, liqueurs can, in fact, be made using any spirit base, from rum to gin, whisky to tequila. While each of these spirits possesses a profile produced by its base distillate – rum starts as molasses, tequila as agave – in a liqueur, these base spirits are a vehicle, not the focus. The deft application of sugar and the choice of botanicals transform that distillate into something far more than the sum of its parts.

Over many centuries, distillation and manufacturing, as well as a more consumer-orientated society, evolved, jumpstarting the transition from prophylactic tonics to recreational pleasures. Then, in the 1500s, the European Age of Exploration created trade routes around the globe, unlocking access to exotic fruits and spices, which would soon be married with alcohol and sugar. Politics, too, had an indirect hand in liqueur's western journey. When Italian aristocrat Catherine de' Medici married the French king Henry II, she brought her taste for her country's liqueurs with her to France. As Pierre Duplais records in his 1866 book *Traité de la fabrication des liqueurs et de la distillation des alcools* (A Treatise on the Manufacture and Distillation of Alcoholic Liquors), Catherine's court

> attracted into France a great number of Italians, who brought along with them the delicate dishes used in their own country and gave instruction as to the methods of preparing them. They were the first who manufactured and sold fine liqueurs in Paris.

In the ensuing centuries, changes to Europe's and – after expansion to the New World – America's socio-economic structures laid the groundwork for broader commercial liqueur production. With the end of feudalism, society stratified, slowly evolving into a model influenced by revolution, industrialization and technological advances. The emerging middle class benefited greatly from all these changes. Not only did more

Carl Larsson, *Getting Ready for a Game*, 1901, oil on canvas. In the background, the woman is reaching for a liqueur bottle that appears to be Bénédictine.

The Skyeman

No. 1　　　　MONDAY, APRIL 24, 1893　　　　PRICE 1ᵈ

THE BIRTHPLACE OF DRAMBUIE

Broadford hotelier registers liqueur at Trademarks Office

For well over a 100 years Drambuie has been produced commercially and is now exported to over 100 countries worldwide. Wherever this classic Highland liqueur is enjoyed it is famous not only for the unique taste and golden colour, but also for its romantic link with Scotland's dramatic past.

The beginnings of this remarkable business venture began right here on the Isle of Skye, with the enterprise of one man, James Ross [pictured left]. Apart from serving the local community of southern Skye on various boards he was a well respected local businessman and farmer who ran the Broadford Hotel in the late nineteenth and early twentieth century.

Several years before, an old recipe had been given to his father by a family friend and James had eventually decided to try and make it up. The recipe is understood to have originally come from a French officer who was part of the retinue of Charles Edward Stuart during the unsuccessful attempt on the throne which ended at the battle of Culloden in 1746.

A NEW LIQUEUR IS BORN

For many years James had been refining and perfecting the liqueur at the hotel, changing the original brandy base to whisky, and experimenting with the recipe until it was finally to his liking.

In April 1893, with the hearty approval of the local clientele, he decided to trademark the result of all his hard work. And so Drambuie, as he had now decided to call the liqueur, was born and was about to be introduced to a much wider and very appreciative public. ◼

The Skyeman tells the story of Drambuie's origins, 24 April 1893.

people have more money, they had more time to enjoy that money. Soon cordials were available for purchase in stores, and could be served to guests in one's home. Cafés, the most egalitarian of gathering spots, poured these sweet sippers for the cognoscenti as they spouted their lofty ideals. Coffee-houses mixed bowls of punch for group enjoyment. And elegant restaurants listed a selection of liqueurs to be enjoyed before and after a meal.

The ascension of cocktails in the late 1800s provided a consummate vehicle to showcase the transformational, and often defining, power of liqueurs. Prior to this era, they were sipped neat or in communal punches. Suddenly, liqueurs became essential components in mixed drinks, the majority of which had only three or four ingredients. The Martinez would not merit mixing without maraschino. The Knickerbocker would not have your knickers in a twist without curaçao. In time, liqueurs would come to define some of the most iconic cocktails in history. Campari in the Negroni, Bénédictine in the Vieux Carré and Drambuie in the Rusty Nail are but a few examples.

In just the last three decades, the cocktail renaissance, which brought back classic cocktail culture, has led to a resurrection of defunct liqueurs and the refinement of existing ones. Along with these historic liqueurs, intriguing new flavours continue to be released, inspiring the creation of wildly inventive cocktails. While many of these products were once available only in the region in which they were produced, they can now be easily acquired thanks to the global connectivity offered by the Internet.

In drinking any liqueur today, we are sipping the history of spirits itself. Without distillation, there is no spirit; without distillation and sugar, there is no liqueur. Dating back to ancient times, liqueurs are, in a sense, the original recreational spirits, arriving before and providing the basic blueprint for all others. However, this blueprint is more than just a model for production. It illustrates the principal reason we drink all spirits: for enjoyment.

As human beings, we crave pleasure. We seek out experiences that enhance our enjoyment of daily life. And it is in this quest to enjoy life – to discover pleasure in many forms – where liqueur has found a happy home across the centuries. Whether aperitif, digestif or cocktail ingredient, the 'musical air' of which Poncelet so poetically spoke provides pleasure with each sip. In short, liqueur's future is virtually assured by the demands of the human body itself. Sugar plus alcohol quite simply taps into one of our most basic evolutionary desires: the desire to feel good.

Man of Bicorp, a cave painting discovered near Valencia, Spain, is a depiction of early honey gathering, 8000–6000 BCE.

I

Sugar and Spice and All Things Nice

Wine is distilled in wetness and it comes out like rosewater.

Al-Kindi, Arab physician and philosopher

One can only imagine the delight our ancient ancestors must have felt when they first stumbled on the intoxicating effects of alcoholic beverages. We can say 'stumbled' because the first alcoholic drinks would have been created by fermentation, a natural, and often spontaneous, conversion of sugars to alcohol. To early man, fermentation must have seemed like a sort of miracle; even more wondrous, however, is distillation, a process created by man, not nature. Indeed, distillation of the alcohol produced by fermentation bears responsibility for the entire world of spirits that we know today. Among these spirits is the hero of our story – liqueur.

While all liqueurs are alcoholic spirits, not all alcoholic spirits are liqueurs. The transformative and crucial ingredient – the great differentiator, as it were – is sweetener in some form. Granted, without a base spirit, there would be no liqueur at all, but it is the addition of sugar (and various botanical accents) that produces such sweet, seductive nectar.

Sweet Salt

Humankind discovered the sensation of sweetness long before we stumbled upon fermentation and, later, invented distillation. In his book *The Story of the Human Body: Evolution, Health, and Disease* (2014), Harvard professor of evolutionary biology Daniel Lieberman points out that our natural predisposition towards sweet flavours can be traced back to our early hominid ancestors. As our closest evolutionary relation, apes evolved a preference for sweetness because sweet foods provided immediate energy as well as helped store fat, both of which were key to survival in periods of food scarcity. Like our primate forebears, human babies have an innate craving for sweet foods because their bodies recognize that sugar offers quick energy. So, if you have a sweet tooth, blame the apes.

Whether in the form of sucrose from sugar cane and sugar beet or fructose from fruit and honey, sugar separates liqueur from liquor. So, just as the story of gin must include juniper and that of of rum must discuss molasses, understanding the origin of liqueur requires a quick history lesson in the evolution of sugars in the human diet. Honey is the oldest known sweetener; its actual harvest can be traced back to somewhere between 8000 and 6000 BCE, as illustrated in the Man of Bicorp, a rock painting created near Valencia, Spain. In parallel to the historical gathering and harvesting of honey, there is evidence of the use of sugar's unrefined form, sugar cane. DNA samples dating to around 8000 BCE suggest that cane grew on the island of Papua New Guinea, where the Indigenous Peoples chewed it in its raw, unprocessed state. In the succeeding centuries, seafarers from the region took these cane crops and cultivation practices to East Asia and India.

When Darius I of Persia invaded India around 518 BCE and came upon sugar cane, he immediately recognized its inherent value. He is said to have called it 'the reed which gives honey without bees'. (The phrase has likewise been attributed to Alexander the Great's admiral Nearchus.) Like the kid in the proverbial candy store, Darius promptly took the bee-less reed home, spreading its cultivation and use throughout the Persian Empire, which stretched from India and Egypt to the Aegean Sea.

While Persia never managed to conquer Greece, Greece benefited from Persia's sweet treasure, using it in medicinal beverages to great effect. In the first century CE, Greek physician and botanist Dioscorides described sugar in his five-volume *De materia medica*, noting its health-giving properties:

> There is a kind of coalesced honey called sugar found in reeds in India and Arabia ... similar in consistency to salt and brittle [enough] to be broken between the teeth like salt. It is good dissolved in water for the intestines and stomach, and taken as a drink to help a painful bladder and kidneys.

For our purposes, the essential phrases above are 'dissolved in water' and 'taken as a drink'. These medicinal practices, coupled with the need to disguise bitter flavours in health-promoting tonics, later influenced the practice of sugaring medicine, which, in turn, evolved into cordials, the earliest form of liqueurs.

While the Arab world was already growing, refining and cooking with sugar by 650 CE, Western Europe's sweet tooth had to be content with honey for almost five hundred years more. It was not until 1099 and the First Crusade, a holy war pitting Western Christians against Eastern Muslims, that soldiers brought this 'sweet salt' further West. Even then, the cost of the sweetener restricted its consumption to the wealthy, all of whom wanted it. The independent Italian Republic of Venice, which

Anonymous engraving of sugar production, *c.* 16th century.

had established strong economic ties with various regions in the Muslim world, became ground zero for sugar export to Western Europe. Venetian merchants saw such value in this white gold that they built a dedicated sugar warehouse in 966 CE in order to export sugar to Central and Eastern Europe.

Sugar cane and the process of refining it were serendipitous discoveries that proved essential to the creation of liqueur. But before liqueur could even exist, a much more complex discovery needed to be made – the process of distillation. Whereas sugar is the key differentiator between liqueurs and all other spirits, distillation is what separates fermented – that is, non-distilled – drinks from spirits. In all probability, human beings stumbled upon the process of fermentation; it occurs naturally when hungry yeast eats sugar, thus producing alcohol. In contrast, distillation requires not only an apparatus to transform fermented liquid into a spirit with a higher alcohol content, but the skill to do so. In its earliest incarnations, distillation was steeped in mysticism, and the cordials that distillation produced possessed an equally preternatural allure.

'Burning Water'

Today most historians concur that the road to modern distillation was ensured when ninth-century Arab alchemists refined the alembic still. Many alchemists were also doctors and pharmacologists who thought that gold had health-giving properties. In their minds, the transmutation of gold was a medicinal means to a spiritual end: eternal life. The conduit through which alchemists sought to achieve immortality was the 'philosopher's stone', most likely not a stone but rather a mystical powder or tincture. From this tincture, one could theoretically produce an 'elixir of life'. The name of this mystical tonic would become known by the interchangeable terms *aqua ardens* (burning water) and *aqua vitae* (water of life). As such, it comes as no surprise that this elixir was the brass, or perhaps we should say golden, ring on the medical carousel.

The idea of transmuted, potable gold, known as *aurum potabile*, opened the door to consumption of these tinctures for one's health, even if immortality was not on the cards. In fact, the supposed benefits of potable gold would hold sway well into the sixteenth century; distillers continued to add it to liqueurs such as the Italian *acqua d'oro* (water of gold) and *rosolio*, which was flavoured with ingredients that might include citrus, spices and rose petals. Indeed, the 1606 proprietary recipe used for Danziger Goldwasser liqueur still includes 22-carat gold leaf.

While Europe floundered amid a dearth of scientific advances, the Arabs flourished in the Islamic Golden Age (800–1258 CE), during which they refined the methods of distillation that they had learned from the Egyptians and the

A modern Danziger Goldwasser advertisement.

Greeks. While the philosopher's stone was the original, ephemeral goal, the Arabs soon recognized that their distilled spirit – coupled with their more advanced distilling apparatus – could better extract and preserve the essential oils present in plants, flowers and herbs than other methods. This, in turn, allowed for the production of a variety of useful products, including medicines, disinfectants, perfumes and dyes. While the Arabs did not invent distillation – the rudimentary process likely dates back to the fifth century BCE – we can unequivocally say that they refined it and, in doing so, planted the seeds for all spirit-based liqueur production.

The Persian polymath and alchemist Jābir ibn Ḥayyān (721–815 CE), known in the West as Geber, was first out of the gate in the ninth century. He sought to separate this higher proof 'spirit' from wine via condensation. To do so, he improved upon the bain-marie still (invented by alchemist Maria the

A simple, layered Pousse-Café with a holiday theme: green crème de menthe, red cinnamon schnapps and clear peppermint schnapps.

Jābir ibn Ḥayyān (Geber), *The Three Books on Alchemy* (1531 edn).

Jewess) to create the alembic, on which all modern stills are based. Jābir's equally accomplished successor al-Razi, or Rhazes (*c.* 854 to 932–5 CE), can be credited with producing ethanol, the type of alcohol from which all spirits are made. He called it *al-kohl* (or *al-kuhul*) of wine, 'kohl' referring to an eye make-up created by converting a solid mineral to a vapour and then to a powder. Eventually, the term became synonymous with anything that was distilled, evolving from *al-kohl* to 'alcohol'.

Unlike Geber or Rhazes, al-Kindi (*c.* 801–873 CE), who we know observed that 'wine is distilled in wetness and it comes out like rosewater', eschewed alchemy, focusing on what distillation could tangibly accomplish. The title of al-Kindi's *The Book of the Chemistry of Perfume and Distillations* speaks for itself. His book contains over one hundred recipes, many of which were likely adopted by the West to serve as the basis for later consumable liqueurs. Following al-Kindi was the philosopher and physician Ibn Sīnā, known as Avicenna (980–1037 CE). The good doctor was more focused on treatments than flavour, and he specifically explored medical cures for heart trouble in his *Medicamento cordialia*. The term *cordialia*, plural of *cordialis*, which, as mentioned, comes from the Latin root *cordis*, or 'heart', evolved evolved into the term 'cordial' – an early name for liqueur that was medicinal in nature. In the modern era, the term 'cordial' is often used interchangeably with the word 'liqueur'. However, in the UK, a 'cordial' has come to denote a non-alcoholic syrup or drink, such as Rose's Lime Cordial.

In the seventh century, when the Islamic world expanded west, Arab knowledge gradually became accessible throughout the Mediterranean, especially in Muslim Spain and Italy. In the southern Italian city of Salerno, the Schola Medica Salernitana (Medical School of Salerno), which was established in the ninth century, benefited from these techniques. It is here that we find some of the first records describing a more advanced form of fractional distillation, which results in a higher-proof, more refined distillate. In the case of liqueur, a concentrated and purified base spirit allows for the true flavours of the botanicals to shine through.

One of the earliest recipes from the Schola was put forth by Italian alchemist Magister Salernus (d. 1167). Salernus used the name *aqua ardens* to describe how 'a mixture of pure and very strong wine with three parts salt, distilled in the usual vessel, produces a liquid which will flame up when set on fire.' The term *aqua ardens* literally translates to 'burning water', similar to

the later Dutch term *brandewijn*, or 'burned wine'. This same 'burned wine' would be the base for the earliest cordials and liqueurs produced in the Netherlands and beyond.

Spain, parts of which were under Arab Muslim influence until 1492, contributed to the further evolution of distillation and liqueur in the form of Catalan physician Arnaldus de

Officina Profumo-Farmaceutica di Santa Maria Novella, Italy's oldest pharmacy and one of the oldest in the world, established in 1221.

Villanova. Returning to the quest for the philosopher's stone, Villanova produced his own spirit and promptly pronounced, 'We call it aqua vitae and this name is remarkably suitable, since it is really a water of immortality.' Despite the misguided idea that aqua vitae was the Fountain of Youth, Villanova and his student Raymond Lull (*c*. 1232–1316) had created the first known medicinal tonic made from spirits. As described in Pierre Duplais' *Treatise*, Villanova and Lull dubbed their cordial *Eau Divine et Admirable* ('Divine and Admirable Water'). While it originally was composed of only brandy and sugar, *Eau Divine* eventually came to be flavoured with lemon, rose and orange flowers.

Beyond schools of medicine, cordial tonics started to spread to Christian monasteries where the ancient skills of the Arabs and Greeks continued to be preserved. The first monastic orders to do this were in Italy, whence the earliest Western liqueurs would arise. In 1221 Dominican friars built a monastery just outside the city of Florence. What would become the Officina Profumo-Farmaceutica di Santa Maria Novella provided medicine and later perfumes and liqueurs to those who could afford them. Nearby, the rolling hills of Tuscany offered a home to the Benedictine abbey of Monte Oliveto Maggiore, founded in 1313. It was known for its Flora di Monteoliveto, which was infused with 23 herbs and aged for six months. Recognizing the need to treat all manner of illnesses, these men of God sourced healing herbs from their environs and created extensive gardens full of medicinal flora.

By the fourteenth century, the seeds of the liqueur industry had been planted in Italy, thanks to distilling knowledge from the Muslim world. With the arrival of the Age of Exploration, the growing cadre of distillers across Europe would have more and more access to spices and sugar.

The Age of Spice

If distillation is the foundation of liqueur, and if sugar is the house, so to speak, spices and various other botanicals are the furniture. Without them, your house is empty. Evidence of spice usage in the East is found in many ancient medical texts from the Egyptian *Ebers Papyrus* (*c.* 1550 BCE) to the sixth-century BCE Sanskrit treatise *Sushruta Samhita*. Among the spices listed are cinnamon, nutmeg, cubeb peppers and cardamom. All of these eventually found their way into medicinal cordials and, later, recreational ones such as rosolio, kümmel and Chartreuse.

In the fifth century BCE, Darius I of Persia had established a roughly 2,500-kilometre (1,500 mi.) route known as the Royal Road, which linked present-day Iran to an area in modern Turkey and, later, to Mesopotamia and Egypt. Many of the roads that made up this route were incorporated into the more famous Silk Road, which was officially opened up during the

The carnivorous *Drosera rotundifolia*, the round-leaved sundew, is thought to be the original base of the ancient rosolio liqueur.

Han Dynasty. Now generally referred to as the Silk Routes, these roads linked China with Central Asia and continued through India, the Arab world and eventually Greece.

These roads were used not only for commerce; they served as hubs for cultural and intellectual exchange. On the darker side, they unwittingly transported disease, such as the plague. They were the first step, albeit a far removed one, towards a modern global economy, having a lasting effect on our knowledge base, trade routes and customs. Despite the term 'silk' in the name, these interconnected thoroughfares – over both land and sea – transported far more than silk. The passages moved spices back and forth: cloves from China, ginger from Southeast Asia, cinnamon from Ceylon (present-day Sri Lanka), cardamom and pepper from India, and nutmeg from the Spice Islands were some of the more valuable examples.

The Muslim world had controlled the maritime spice routes in the Persian Gulf since the fourth century CE, eventually commandeering ports in Muslim-influenced southern Spain, as well as in the independent rival cities of Venice and Genoa on the Italian peninsula. This widespread Arab-Muslim influence in Europe – economic, political and social – did not sit well with the Catholic Church. Hungry to regain the Holy Land from those deemed infidels, the Church launched the Crusades, which lasted from 1095 to 1291.

The Crusades were, unwittingly, a turning point for the future of liqueur, for three seemingly conflicting reasons: luxury, medicine and religion. When Western European soldiers returned home with sugar and spices, they exposed a broader swathe of Northern Europe to these exotic and rare delicacies, as well as information on how to use them for medicine and preservation. Spices such as pepper were so highly prized that they were often used as currency to pay rent, taxes and dowries. In England, the phrase 'he hath no pepper' was a polite way of saying that the pepper-less 'he' in question was, colloquially, a loser.

With Spanish and Italian ports serving as the main conduits to Eastern riches, Western Europeans wanted more direct access to and more control of the spices they craved. Then, in 1453, the Ottoman Empire took Constantinople, renaming it Istanbul. Straddling the continents of Europe and Asia, Istanbul gave the Ottomans an indisputable advantage in the Mediterranean. While they did not cut off the spice routes, they did levy exorbitant taxes on the spices themselves.

Even though wealthy Europeans could pay the prices demanded, they surely did not want to. What they did want, though, was the social standing that spices – and everything they flavoured – symbolized. In order to supplant the Arab dominance of the spice trade, Western Europe zealously embarked on a period that Niall Ferguson dubs the 'spice race' in his book *Civilization: The West and the Rest* (2011).

While Italy was the first country to produce Western liqueurs, it had a relatively peripheral presence during the several

Spices that found their way into liqueurs. Upper row from left to right: cinnamon, star anise, ginger, mace; centre: fennel seeds, green cardamom; lower row: coriander, aniseed, cloves, allspice, nutmeg.

centuries of feverish oceanic exploration. This era of discovery was unquestionably a game for countries situated on the Atlantic coast, which Italy most assuredly was not. Italy may not have manned the ships, but Italian explorers such as Christopher Columbus and Amerigo Vespucci would play vital roles when they sailed under the banners of Spain and Portugal, respectively.

Portugal set to sea first, eager to control spices, including sugar, which was regarded as a spice at this time. As early as 1418, Portuguese sailors discovered one of the islands in the Madeira archipelago; Prince Henry the Navigator quickly introduced sugar cane there, gaining a huge trading advantage. Some decades later in 1498, Vasco da Gama charted the first eastern trade route to India, gaining access to sugar and other spices. Then, in 1500, Pedro Cabral accidentally discovered Brazil when he was blown far off course on his way to India. On the journey, he brought sugar cane, which flourished in the Brazilian climate, and helped establish the crop in the Western Hemisphere. (By 1625, Brazil would supply most of Europe with sugar.) Having embarked on the colonization of Brazil, the Portuguese set their sights on the Spice Islands, whose location was closely guarded by the Arabs. While Portugal had access to Indian spices, the explorers and merchants wanted to control the spice trade completely. The Spice Islands, known collectively as Maluku, or the Moluccas, were the sole sources of nutmeg, mace, cloves and pepper. Despite the Arabs' secrecy, the location of the islands was ascertained in 1512 by Portugal, thanks to information that had been received from sailors in Malacca, a port city at the bottom of the Malay Peninsula. Portuguese sailors followed this up with the discovery of Ceylon in 1518. Ceylon was home to cinnamon. With control of the Spice Islands and Ceylon, Portugal cemented its monopoly of the spice trade, delivering pepper, cloves, nutmeg, mace and cinnamon to Europe without the burden of a middleman.

Not to be outdone, Spanish explorers scrambled to compete, starting in 1492. Hired by Ferdinand II and Isabella I of Spain, Christopher Columbus set sail across the Atlantic, hoping to discover a western route to Asia. Instead, he ran smack into the Americas, specifically the island that would later become the Dominican Republic and Haiti, naming it Hispaniola. Columbus brought sugar cane with him, leading the way for the Spanish sugar industry to spread throughout its Caribbean colonies.

St. Elizabeth
Allspice Dram.

In 1494 Columbus's second voyage sent him to Jamaica, where he encountered allspice, which joined cinnamon, cloves and other spices in sixteenth-century European cuisine and cordials. Known as *pimienta de Jamaica* (Jamaican pepper) in Spanish, the British dubbed it 'allspice' due to the fact that it combined the character of cinnamon, nutmeg and anise. All-spice is the central component of pimento dram, a rum-based liqueur produced in Jamaica that would become a frequent component in tiki drinks during the twentieth century.

Settlements such as Hispaniola and Jamaica would lay the foundations for the 'triangular trade', which lasted from the sixteenth to the nineteenth century. This brutal system trans-ported African slaves to the Americas to work on sugar (and various other) plantations, which, in turn, produced rum and other goods for export to Europe and Africa.

Other Sweet Treasures

While Columbus is perhaps the best known of Spain's mari-ners, Alonso de Ojeda could be considered far more important for the future of liqueur. In 1499 Ojeda colonized an island that would come to be called Curaçao. The Spanish settlers planted sweet Valencia orange trees that they had brought from the home country, only to discover that they produced inedible fruit. The island's inhospitable growing conditions transmogri-fied the Valencia orange into a varietal now known as the laraha.

The colonists found these new oranges far too acidic and harsh for eating, effectively abandoning the crop. The Spaniards' loss was the Netherlands' gain. Dutch explorers, who attacked the Spanish and won control of the island in 1634, discovered that the bitter peels, when dried, were immensely aromatic. This bitterness, balanced with the addition of sugar, provided an

The fruit of the laraha orange tree.

optimal base for the orange liqueur known as curaçao. The first commercial curaçao liqueur was, not surprisingly, produced in the Netherlands. Today, curaçao and its Gallic cousin triple sec play primary roles in hundreds of classic cocktails, making these orange liqueurs almost indispensable behind the bar.

Adding to these flavourful riches, the Spanish conquistador Hernán Cortés arrived in Mexico in 1519. There it is said that the Aztecs served Cortés and his men an exotic drink of chocolate, made from cacao beans and vanilla. While some stories suggest Columbus had discovered cacao and vanilla back in 1502, Cortés took the products back to Europe. The novel flavours captured the fancy of the wealthy and, in turn, made their way into liqueurs. Cacao would later define crème de cacao, whose flavour is more like vanilla and cocoa than typical chocolate. This crème liqueur is essential in sweet cocktails such as the Grasshopper, the Alexander and the Pink Squirrel. Vanilla would find its way into liqueurs such as Tuaca and Baileys Irish Cream.

Man carrying a cacao pod, Aztec, 1440–1521. Drinking chocolate was already enjoyed by the Aztecs when Cortés arrived.

Cortés's felicitous gustatory discovery came at an enormous cost to the Aztecs. The Spanish brought disease and war to the Indigenous population, leading to their eventual eradication. The fall of the Aztec Empire is but one example of the dark side of expansion, which was fuelled, among other things, by the European demand for exotic luxury goods.

While Spain and Portugal profited massively from their early explorations, their fortunes would not last. In 1580 Portugal grappled with a dynastic crisis that opened the door for Spain to assimilate its neighbour, effectively crippling Portugal's power over the seas. But misfortune would soon fall upon

Spain, too. Determined to return the newly Protestant English back to their former Catholicism, Spain led its fleet towards the island nation. The recently converted Protestant Dutch, who were under equal pressure from Spain, fought by the side of England. In 1588 the Dutch and English resoundingly defeated the Spanish Armada. This victory presaged the Netherlands' seventeenth-century trade dominance and would facilitate the country's emergence as one of the earliest and most influential commercial liqueur producers. But, by the next century, the Dutch would be supplanted by the English, who would build an empire on which the sun never set.

Title page from an early 16th-century edition of Hieronymus Brunschwig's second work on distillation, *Liber de arte distillandi de compositis* (On the Art of Distilling Compounds).

2
Information, Individuality and Independence

Whosoever commands the sea commands the trade;
whosoever commands the trade of the world commands
the riches of the world, and consequently the world itself.
Sir Walter Raleigh (*c.* 1552–1618), 'A Discourse of the Invention
of Ships, Anchors, Compass'

Although movable type had been invented by the Chinese around 1040 CE, Johannes Gutenberg's printing press revolutionized the accessibility of information in the West when it was introduced in 1450. Inexpensive, mass-produced books printed in the vernacular soon supplanted cost-prohibitive, arduously hand-copied books, chiefly written in rarefied Latin. Whether the Bible or a world atlas, a political treatise or a recipe book, printed materials allowed knowledge to be shared. And that knowledge gave birth to new, even heretical, ideas about the world and man's place in it.

In 1500, not long after Gutenberg established his press, the first printed guide to distilling medicinal tonics had arrived courtesy of the German surgeon Hieronymus Brunschwig. *Liber de arte distillandi de simplicibus* (On the Art of Distillation Out of Simple Ingredients) was written for the layman, and Brunschwig specifically singled out the common people as his readership. Among the 250-plus recipes for various medicinal 'waters' are many ingredients used in modern liqueurs, such as 'flowres sambuci or eldre' (elderflowers), used in St-Germain, 'hasselnuttys' (hazelnuts), used in Frangelico, and 'blacke beryes', used in crème de mûre. Further, he made a point of noting that sweetening the cordials made them more palatable. The popularity of Brunschwig's book foreshadowed a flowering of recipe book culture, which played a crucial role in the accessibility and standardization of liqueur recipes.

Brunschwig's flowers, nuts and berries might seem inconsequential in relation to Luther's religious treatise, but they are both part of a seismic shift in perception. Recipe books not only

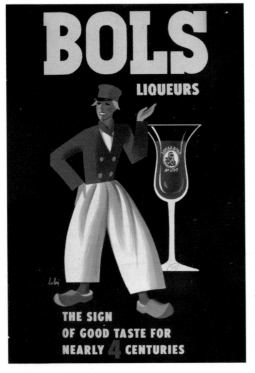

Advertisement for Bols. Founded in 1575 in Amsterdam, Bols is the oldest extant distillery brand.

helped people define their cultural identity – just as Luther made them question their religious identity – but enabled literate people, high- and low-born alike, to possess and act upon knowledge. Man, it seemed, was not just a pawn in the game of life. This philosophy of Humanism blossomed across Europe, setting the stage for massive social change. As Luther rocked the religious world, a new breed of Humanist philosopher challenged people to recognize that men controlled their own lives and that rational thinking should be used to solve life's problems.

The Reformation and the rise of Humanism forcefully pushed people to question their world: 'Who am I?' 'What is my place in the universe?' 'Does God rule over me, or am I my own master?' With each of these questions – whether religious, moral or personal – man moved towards a future that celebrated the individual. This was the ground-breaking moment in society that would help transform liqueur from a medicinal necessity to a seductive pleasure.

The Liqueur-ious Low Countries

As a result of direct trade with the Arab world in the early Middle Ages, Italy was the first Western country to distil cordials. By the 1400s, however, the people of the Low Countries – a historic region that encompassed the Netherlands, Belgium, Luxembourg and parts of Germany and France – were also well schooled in the art of distillation and the application of spices. In fact, a Middle Dutch manuscript from the fifteenth century focused on making *brandewijn*, also known as burnt wine, which hearkens back to the 'burning water' known as *aqua ardens*. The modern equivalent term for burnt wine would be 'brandy'. In the 1600s *brandewijn* served as the spirit base for the Dutch (and Belgian) juniper spirit known as genever. The forefather of – but not to be confused with – gin, genever is characterized by a whisky-like flavour and a complex balance of botanicals.

Because Spain's King Philip II was also king of the Netherlands through marriage, the people of the Low Countries were Spanish subjects. Despite being under the thumb of Catholic Spain, many of the Dutch had started to eschew Catholicism and embrace Calvinism, an emerging branch of Protestantism that would also spread to England and then to the American colonies. In 1568 Philip denounced these Protestant Netherlanders as heretics and established a Dutch Inquisition, which waged a particularly brutal campaign against the Dutch people. If ever there was a cause for war, this was it. The Dutch provinces banded together and engaged the Spanish in the Eighty Years War (1568–1648). By 1581 they had won independence, becoming the Seven United Netherlands (also called the Seven Provinces) and setting the stage for the prosperous Dutch Golden Age.

Newly independent, the Dutch set sail in 1596, determined to win control of the lucrative spice routes. They returned from the Eastern spice routes with a bountiful cargo, which lit a fire under the newly emerging, profit-hungry merchant class. In 1602, to make competition between merchants fair and equitable, the government established the Verenigde Oost-Indische Compagnie (VOC), or Dutch East India Company. With the growing demand for spices at home and the determination to own the supply routes, the VOC went after the Portuguese-dominated Spice Islands, sparking the Dutch–Portuguese War (1602–63). At the end of the war, the Dutch had taken control of the former Portuguese-held possessions in East and South Asia.

The VOC's successes in the East encouraged the formation of the Geoctrooieerde Westindische Compagnie (GWC), or

Dutch West India Company, in 1621. Along with the West Indies, the GWC participated in the Atlantic slave trade, as well as operating in Brazil and the Americas. In order to hamper the Portuguese and Spanish trade monopoly in the West, the GWC devised a *Groot Desseyn* (Grand Design).

In 1630, at the midpoint of the Dutch–Portuguese War, the GWC gained control of the lucrative Portuguese sugar and slave trade in Brazil. Despite continued skirmishes with the Portuguese, the Dutch controlled the sugar cane plantations there until the mid-1600s. During this period, they also operated approximately fifty sugar refineries in Amsterdam, from which they controlled both the refining and sale of sugar in Europe. Although they were finally pushed out of Brazil by the Portuguese in 1654, the Dutch maintained their monopoly on sugar for a quarter of a century, thus greatly aiding their burgeoning liqueur industry. Likewise, the Dutch had captured Curaçao from the Spanish in 1634, giving them full access to the island's laraha orange crops, which would become the hallmark of Dutch curaçao liqueur. One of the first – and in relation to

Dried laraha orange peels.

liqueur, most important – companies to profit from the VOC's and the GWC's possessions was Bols, the producer of liqueur and later genever. In 1575 the Bols family had arrived in Amsterdam, where they opened their distillery, dubbing it 't Lootsje. The Bols archives show that the earliest cordials highlighted many of the major spoils of exploration: *kaneel* (cinnamon), *nagel* (clove) and orange curaçao. Other liqueurs included anisette and crème d'anis, and *karwij* (caraway), which is more familiarly known as kümmel. According to Bols historian Ton Vermeulen, the company's *karwij* was made with caraway only; other styles from different companies might contain caraway and cumin, as well as additional botanicals such as fennel and orris root.

Spices such as cloves and cinnamon found their way into Bols's liqueurs thanks in great degree to Lucas Bols's relationship with the VOC. From 1680 to 1719, Bols supplied the VOC's influential board of directors with 'fine waters' to the exclusion of all other distillers; Lucas Bols himself used his position to become a shareholder in the company, which, in turn, gave him prime access to the goods that the ships brought home. Not only did he create hundreds of liqueur recipes, but he enlisted the VOC to distribute Bols's liqueurs internationally.

Not coincidentally, the Netherlands entered its Golden Age one year after the VOC was formed. From 1603 to 1715, the Netherlands emerged as one of the most powerful and wealthy nations in Europe; the populace, which now included the *brede middenstand* (a well-off middle class), reaped the benefits. With luxuries from its colonies flowing into the country, ingredients such as sugar, spices and exotic fruits became commonplace for a large portion of society.

This gustatory opulence, however, posed something of a challenge to this newly emerging country of Protestant Calvinists. So, being an industrious and practical people, they balanced their daily and somewhat plain diet – ample, not ostentatious

The range of Senior & Co's curaçao liqueurs. The company's curaçao is still produced on the island of Curaçao using laraha oranges.

– with boisterous, indulgent celebrations whenever possible. The most common life events called for specific liqueurs to be served. *Kandeel*, a spiced eggnog-style liqueur, commemorated a new birth; the gold leaf-flecked *Bruidstranen*, or Bride's Tears, was sipped at weddings and afterwards to remind the husband of his vows. Old Dutch liqueurs such as these still maintain a presence today.

Empire Building

While the Dutch and their British neighbours shared a common religion, as well as an antagonistic relationship with Spain, they also became the primary competitors for spice in the 1600s. To be fair, both countries were late to the exploration game. In 1492 Columbus set foot in the Americas, and Spain had colonized portions of Mexico, Peru, the Caribbean and Florida. In 1498 Vasco de Gama discovered a route to India; Portugal went on to set up colonies in Brazil, Africa and India, among others.

But, whereas the Netherlands flourished economically and developed a formidable navy during this period, England was woefully behind the curve.

The plague had crippled England's national treasury and decimated the population. Meanwhile, over the next two centuries, ruthless English monarchs waged war after war, among them the Hundred Years War from 1337 to 1453 and the War of the Roses (1455–85). At this time, England was a nation of land armies, unlike the Netherlands, which ruled the seas. Extensive trade and colonization were an afterthought until the reign of Queen Elizabeth I, which began in 1558.

As the head of a newly Protestant country, Elizabeth saw Catholic Spain as a clear and present danger to England's sovereignty. In order to undermine Spain's power, the queen sent men such as Sir Francis Drake and Sir Walter Raleigh to commandeer Iberian treasure ships. In 1587 Drake captured the Portuguese carrack *São Filipe* on its return voyage from the East Indies; its hold was full of gold and spices. A year later, Drake was instrumental in the fall of the Spanish Armada, when its ships attempted to invade England, much as Elizabeth had feared. Not only did Drake help cripple Spain's stranglehold on the Atlantic trade routes, but he managed to acquire essential and secret information about those routes that would be used when the English finally set sail.

In 1592 fellow English swashbuckler-cum-explorer Sir Walter Raleigh built on Drake's successes when he orchestrated the capture of the Portuguese ship *Madre de Deus*. As with the *São Filipe*, the ship's hold was packed with a treasure-trove that included nutmeg, mace and pepper. These riches provided a glimpse into the profits that awaited the Crown. Elizabeth could no longer resist the temptation to venture forth. In 1600, two years before the establishment of the Dutch VOC, the English East India Company (EIC) received a Royal Charter

46

from the queen. (The EIC would become the British East India Company in 1707, when the Act of Union of England and Scotland formed Great Britain.) England's fleet struggled to compete with that of the Netherlands for various reasons, including lack of funding after Elizabeth's death in 1603 and, later, the English Civil Wars from 1642 to 1651. It would be more than a century before the British Navy emerged as the master of the seas in the 1800s.

Despite these issues, England established 'factories', essentially trading hubs, starting in 1603. One of these outposts was on the nutmeg-rich island of Run in Indonesia. While all spices enjoyed a healthy mark-up in Europe, nutmeg was in massively high demand with an equally huge mark-up. Indeed, according to Charles Corn in *The Scents of Eden* (1999), one could purchase nutmeg for a penny a pound on the island of Run. It could then be sold in Europe, by one estimate, at a mark-up of 32,000 per cent. In the seventeenth century, nutmeg was not only

Early 20th-century print published by the nutmeg company Wolters depicting villagers drying nutmeg in the Banda Islands.

considered a plague treatment, but, more importantly, a way for the upper class to flaunt its wealth. The spice found its way into everything from sachets to foods to drinks.

Not to be bested by their neighbours, the Dutch instigated the Nutmeg Wars (1661–7), challenging the English claim to Run, England's last nutmeg holding. In 1667, as part of the negotiations to end the war, the Dutch took possession of Run and ceded a then little-known island in North America to the English. That island is what we now know as Manhattan.

From Craze to Commercialization

Throughout most of the 1500s, the English were primarily a nation of beer drinkers. They did, in fact, employ spices and sugar in their beers and ales, but hard alcohol, such as aqua vitae, was generally reserved for medicine. The 'water of life' was often referred to as *usque-bath*, or Irish aqua vitae. While the word evolved into the modern term 'whiskey'/'whisky', *usque-bath* was originally a sweetened, medicinal cordial water that was flavoured with various herbs and spices in the 1600s.

Thanks to the proliferation of the printing press since 1453, recipes for *usque-bath* and multiple other cordials had become available to various levels of society in the mass-produced recipe books of the day. In Thomas Dawson's *The Good Huswifes Jewell* (1596–7), the 'husewife' of the title referred to a more privileged English woman tasked with running the domestic affairs of the household. Dawson's book provided recipes for various waters in a section titled 'Remedies'. His water of life included sugar, nutmeg and cinnamon, among other ingredients. Suggesting further stratification in social roles, *Delightes for Ladies* (1636) by Hugh Plat was written for women of a higher class. Plat's recipe for *usque-bath* was sweetened with molasses and flavoured with liquorice, anise seeds, cloves, dates and raisins.

For those who did not distil at home, strong water shops had arrived in the 1570s, allowing people to purchase flavoured aqua vitae (often distilled from beer). By 1600 there were approximately two hundred of these shops in London, distilling

Myristica moschata, the aromatic (or true) nutmeg tree. Botanical print published by J. Churchill, London, 1829.

their spirits with whatever they could gather and without any regulation whatsoever. Because of all the competing factions, the role of liqueur in society was still quite broad at this time. E. C. Spary, in *Materials and Expertise in Early Modern Europe* (2010), sums it up well, saying,

> The struggle to capture the meaning of liqueurs, to produce them as objects of consumption and knowledge, went on at commercial, scientific and medical levels . . . because of the fine line between foods, remedies and toiletries, and the fact that all three were purchased by the same clientele.

Quite simply, there were too many cooks in the distilling kitchen for liqueur to lay claim to its primarily recreational role.

In an effort to create clear, public rules for those who distilled and how they did it, a physician named Thomas de Mayerne stepped into the fray. In 1638 he helped establish a professional distillers' organization, governed by set rules and regulations to ensure quality. The Worshipful Company of Distillers was formed and granted the sole right to distil grain within the City of London and Westminster, as well as 34 kilometres (21 mi.) beyond them.

At this time, juniper water, essentially a rough sort of gin, was consumed as a medicine; in his *Diary* (1663), Samuel Pepys mentions sipping this 'water' for stomach troubles. Beer and brandy were the preferred recreational tipples, while rum was not yet in fashion. Then, in 1688, England's alcohol landscape changed drastically, as an indirect result of the religious schism occurring in the country. That year, the Catholic king James II found himself unceremoniously deposed. In what is known as the Glorious Revolution, Dutch Protestant William of Orange, and his English Protestant wife Mary (James's daughter), took the throne. William brought to England his penchant for the malted, juniper spirit called genever.

The nobility quickly fell in line with the king's drink of choice; it became patriotic to drink 'English' booze. To hamper the French economy in wartime, William blocked all English imports of French goods, including brandy. Unfortunately, the lower classes could never afford such a kingly extravagance as finely distilled genever. Desperate to emulate their superiors and searching for a potent panacea to their daily lives, the poor created their own version of genever, which they anglicized to 'gin'. More akin to moonshine than anything else, this deadly spirit was made from ingredients such as oil of vitriol (sulphuric acid) and turpentine in an attempt to approximate genever's botanical juniper character.

From roughly 1720 to the 1770s, a three-decade bender now called the Gin Craze swept across England, especially London. To disguise the unsavoury taste of this poor-man's genever, people sweetened it with sugar, which by this time was both plentiful and affordable to all but the most impoverished souls. The often-sweetened Old Tom style of gin is sometimes referred to as a 'cordial gin', setting the stage for the fruit- and spice-infused gin cordials that became massively popular in the eighteenth and nineteenth centuries.

In the late 1700s, once the Gin Craze was over, a breed of respectable gentlemen gin distillers with now-familiar names – Gordon, Gilbey, Tanqueray and others – arrived on the scene. Between 1820 and 1840, these men formed the Rectifiers Club to ensure quality control and healthy competition on a commercial scale. Some of the first spirits these men produced were gin-based cordials. Today, gin is the unofficial national spirit of England and the base for all of the country's best-known liqueurs, including sloe gin (a style of gin cordial) and the fruit cup.

With a renewed interest in sloe gin, many contemporary evocations are now available. Historic brands like Hayman's, founded in 1863, offer a classic blueprint for style.

As more refined gin became the norm, it became more accepted in polite society and often formed the base spirit for punch. During the eighteenth century, while the lower classes guzzled their bastardized gin punch, the fashionable set gathered around communal punch bowls featuring more sophisticated iterations of the juniper spirit. What was fashionable in England soon became fashionable in the American colonies, whose denizens sought to emulate their continental parents. And, just as punch travelled across the Atlantic, so too did the ideas of the Enlightenment, which took Europe by storm in the late seventeenth century.

From Enlightenment to Rum to Revolution

In 1666, one hundred years and change before the American War of Independence, Englishman Isaac Newton sat down under an apple tree to ponder the mysteries of the universe. As the story goes, an errant apple fell on Newton's noggin, inspiring him to compose his ground-breaking *Philosophiæ naturalis principia mathematica* (Mathematical Principles of Natural Philosophy, 1687). While Newton was a religious man, his rational, scientific process made him an unwitting poster boy for the Enlightenment. A few years later, political philosopher John Locke wrote *The Two Treatises of Civil Government* (1689), which championed the equally rational idea that 'being all equal and independent, no one ought to harm another in his life, health, liberty, or possessions.'

While the English argued over ideas in their coffee-houses and pubs, the colonials enjoyed spirited discussions in the taverns that pervaded every street in every city. These meeting places served as more than bars; they were post offices, banks and trading posts. And it was in these taverns that Enlightenment thinking took wing. There is no better way to get up the courage to present seditious ideas than to lubricate oneself with booze. In fact, colonial folk got downright loquacious. You could say that America was founded on enlightened intoxication.

Beer and cider were the original colonial tipples, but rum soon became the preferred road to inebriation. Along with its obvious stimulating effects, rum provided a 'safe' – and, the colonists thought, healthful – alternative to polluted water. The less fortunate colonists slugged it straight, much as the English lower classes consumed deadly gin during the Craze. The well-to-do, however, enjoyed it in various rum punches and as the base for homemade liqueurs, such as Martha Washington's cherry bounce. Unfortunately, rum and its peripheral uses in other sweet concoctions bring us to one of the darker and more reprehensible parts of liqueur's history, the Triangular Trade.

Prior to revolution and independence, the Colonies still had to kowtow to the British State on the economic front. In relation to liqueur, the cash crop was sugar cane. In England, sugar became an addiction for all levels of society starting in the seventeenth century. Likewise, rum from the West Indies and from New England became a coveted spirit. The British Navy served daily rations of it to its sailors, and people mixed it in rum punch. In the American colonies, rum punches, rum toddies and rum shrubs became the order of the day. Shrubs, in particular, came about due to smuggling, which had started in England during the late 1600s because of luxury taxes on imports. Smugglers stored their rum offshore, where it often became contaminated with sea water. To conceal the foul flavours, people added sugar and fruit to the rum, creating a sort of DIY liqueur.

Historically, the sugar trade is irrevocably linked to the Atlantic slave trade, which dates back to Portugal's transatlantic exportation of Africans to the West. But it is the Triangular Trade through which Great Britain, America and Africa were linked. Molasses from the West Indies was sent to New England, rum was sent to Africa and enslaved people were sent back to the American colonies and to the West Indies, where they frequently worked the sugar plantations.

It is in 1733 that rum, in both its consumption and its production, played a central role in the story of liqueur. That year, the British enacted the Molasses Act, which taxed the import of sugar, molasses and rum from non-British colonies to the American colonies. In 1764 Britain passed the equally prohibitive Sugar Act, aimed at stopping smuggling of the products taxed by the Molasses Act. Finally, Great Britain's American children grew weary of their subservience to King George II.

In taverns across the colonial landscape, Humanistic thinkers such as Benjamin Franklin and Thomas Jefferson drank heartily – probably over bowls of rum punch – and uttered their seditious thoughts.

Santa Maria Novella Alkermes. A favourite of Catherine de' Medici, this liqueur is still produced today.

3
The Road to Enlightenment and Revolution

Man will never be free until the last king is strangled
with the entrails of the last priest.
Attrib. to Denis Diderot, *Les Eleuthéromanes* (1772)

Today the Enlightenment is often considered the philosophical
threshold for modern social and political thought. Whether the
issue at hand was, colloquially, life, liberty or the pursuit of hap-
piness, grand ideas were at the heart of seventeenth- and
eighteenth-century Europe. The culture evolved to accommo-
date the discussion of provocative ideas, creating locales where
people could both gather and debate. Nowhere was this more
apparent than in France, where the *philosophes* – men of letters
like Diderot, Voltaire and Rousseau – held court at aristocratic
Paris salons and egalitarian cafés to deliberate and pontificate. As
ideas flourished, so did liqueur: when people get together and
argue, they are most likely going to need spirituous libations.

When Life Gives You Lemons (and Coffee)

Long before the Enlightenment, Catherine de' Medici had brought her own 'enlightened' views about food, fashion and art to the French court when she married the future King Henry II of France. As characterized by James Mew and John Ashton in their book *Drinks of the World* (1896), the queen-to-be shared 'all the voluptuous discoveries and superfluities of Italy and helped to augment considerably the number of new liqueurs and to popularize their usage'. Catherine's favourite cordial was alchermes (also spelled alkermes), a spiced liqueur whose name stems from the Arabic *al-kirmiz*. While sometimes used medicinally, alchermes was also enjoyed as an aphrodisiac, illustrating a more recreational role as well.

To satisfy her passion for alchermes and other Italian cordials, Catherine brought court distillers with her to France. They, in turn, introduced Florentine recipes and Italian distilling techniques, thus laying the foundation for France's refined and indispensable contributions to the world of liqueur. But Catherine and her alchermes were not the only Italian imports.

Lemonade had made its way to France and the rest of Europe via Italy, where lemonade-sellers served the tart thirst-quencher out of tanks carried on their backs. French vendors enthusiastically imitated their Italian counterparts, but would soon take lemonade to an entirely new level. Signalling lemonade's seventeenth-century popularity, chef François Pierre La Varenne included a lemonade recipe in *Le Cuisinier françois* (The French Cook, 1651), today considered one of the primary cookbooks that defined modern French cooking. Indeed, the popularity of the beverage unwittingly helped Paris escape the ravages of the 1668 plague to a large degree: the preponderance of lemon rinds in the city's trash created an utterly inhospitable home for the disease-ridden fleas that hopped a ride on wandering rats.

Not so coincidentally, the proprietor of Le Procope, Paris's oldest café, was a Sicilian lemonade-seller named Procopio Cutò. Le Procope opened its doors in 1686 and would become one of the primary gathering places for *philosophes* such as Voltaire and Diderot, whose ideas were instrumental in the gestation of the French Revolution. As a concept, the café was very much of its time. As noted earlier, the continued emergence of new ideas demanded a place for those ideas to be discussed. The café offered the ideal spot for just such discussions, as well as an excuse to linger over liqueurs, lemonade and coffee, which had arrived in Europe in the 1600s.

Moreover, the café appeared at a crucial time in France's history. As with much of Europe, France had faced massive upheaval in the wake of the Black Death: Paris alone lost approximately one-third of its inhabitants to the plague. Further loss of life occurred during the Hundred Years War with England. These two events resulted in fewer labourers, who – in an extreme case of demand exceeding supply – were able to make more money for their work. Further, feudal society was gradually being replaced with a multiple-tier class system, allowing diverse types of people to open up new markets and produce more products. People moved to the cities, where they were exposed to a more dynamic cultural milieu in which they could spend their money.

Today the term 'café' (or *caffè* in Italian) is inextricably linked to coffee. However, to a certain degree, the café's origins began with liqueur. In France, the privilege of distilling aqua vitae, essentially brandy, belonged to the apothecaries until the sixteenth century. Over the next century, groups as varied as the vinegar-makers and the victuallers (those who ran eating establishments) were granted the right to distil. In 1676 these distillers officially merged with the *limonadiers* (lemonade-sellers) as a single guild, an organization that grouped artisans

Lemonade merchant, 1771, hand-coloured etching, from vol. 1 of Mary and Matthew Darly's *24 Caricatures by Several Ladies Gentleman Artists &c.* The print makes a mockery of the French, embodied in this lemonade seller decked out in wooden sabots and a bearskin hat.

FRENCH-LEMONADE-MERCHANT.

based on their trade in order to offer them economic advantages. As the seventeenth century wound down, and the guild became more influential, limonadiers ditched their tanks and began to sell their drinks from small beverage carts. These carts evolved into limonadier shops, which eventually became known as cafés. And, while 'café' in French translates as 'coffee', the earliest cafés were specifically sit-down establishments that served lemonade, coffee and liqueurs.

By the eighteenth century, the Compagnie de Limonadiers became one of the richest and most influential guilds in France. Not surprisingly, the number of limonadier shops rose exponentially. In the early 1700s, there were around three hundred cafés in Paris alone; by the end of the century, the numbers (depending on the source) ran from eight hundred to more than 2,000, catering to a wide variety of teetotalling and bibulous needs. While multiple groups, including apothecaries, merchants and perfumers, had the right to distil alcohol, the limonadiers had the sole right to sell their spirits to customers in a seated environment.

In the *Dictionnaire portatif des arts et métiers* (Portable Dictionary of Arts and Crafts, 1766), author Philippe Macquer records that the limonadiers were given the privilege of selling a broad range of stimulants, including 'all the strong ratafias and table liqueurs'. At the time, 'ratafia' was a catch-all term for fruit-based liqueurs, although ratafias had originally been made specifically from the stones of fruit like peaches and cherries. In 1728 François Guislier Du Verger, in his *Traité des liqueurs, esprits ou essences, et la manière de s'en servir utilement* (Treatise on Liqueurs, Spirits or Essences, and the Manner of Using

'La Belle Limonadiere', 1816, hand-coloured etching.

Them Usefully), had labelled ratafias as *liqueurs de conversation*. In Verger's words, these 'conversation liqueurs' were noteworthy for the fact that 'One can drink four or six little glasses without getting drunk.' The use of the term 'conversation' and the fact that these liqueurs would not incapacitate you (thus allowing for prolonged sociability) suggests that liqueurs were being enjoyed in convivial situations.

While Guislier's observations appear related to more privileged groups, Jacques-François Demachy's *L'Art du distillateur liquoriste* (1775) suggests that liqueurs could be accessed by everyone, albeit of varying quality. According to the author, the same liqueur could be 'fine, or bourgeois, or common'; its quality was affected by the amount of eau de vie or sugar, as well as the choice of fruit. Among the liqueur recipes he offered were a cassis-based ratafia, as well as *eau divine*, *eau de thé*, *liqueurs de Barbade* and various rosoli (the plural of rosolio).

Signalling the continued importance of the limonadiers, the manual *L'Art du limonadier* (The Art of the Limonadier) was released in 1804. Written by limonadiers for limonadiers, it defined the artisan's role not only as host of his establishment and purveyor of chocolate, tea and coffee, but as *distillateur* producing *les meilleurs liqueurs* (the best liqueurs). The chapter regarding *les liqueurs spiriteuses*, meaning those using an alcohol base, consumes 86 pages of this 281-page book. Of the 73 recipes in the chapter, there are 22 for ratafia, several versions of noyau (originally a ratafia made from the kernels of stone fruits) and maraschino, as well as various rosoli di Torino, *scubac* (the Scottish escubac) and Parfait Amour.

Along with the café society established by the limonadiers, Paris also played host to a vital, albeit more aristocratic, institution known as the salon. As the unofficial clubhouse of the Enlightenment, the salon offered a social environment for stimulating and sometimes subversive discourse. While women did not always participate in the discussions, they were the ones who organized and hosted the gatherings, as well as those who chose what topics to explore. Moreover, the upper middle class, known as the bourgeoisie, could hobnob with the aristocrats and the *philosophes*, creating a pivotal expansion of the public social sphere.

This evolving world was the cradle into which future French master liqueurist Marie Brizard was born, giving her the opportunity to make a mark in an arena dominated by men. Comparable in some ways to Lucas Bols, Brizard influenced commercial liqueur production in France and exported her products abroad.

As the daughter of Pierre Brizard, a cooper and master distiller, Marie was no stranger to the world of spirits. However, it was not until 1750 that she stumbled into the world of liqueurs when a sickly West Indian sailor gifted her a recipe for aniseed liqueur as a tangible *merci beaucoup* for nursing him back to health. Being female, Brizard was forbidden from owning a business (Enlightened thinking did have its boundaries), but this never deterred her. She simply enlisted the assistance of Jean-Baptiste Roger in order to form Maison Marie Brizard & Roger. In 1763 Marie finally perfected her recipe for the company's flagship anisette liqueur, which became a fixture at the court of Louis XV; three years later, she would release her version of Parfait Amour, which is still one of the company's marquee brands.

The Brizard brand was followed by multiple others whose products arrived and thrived by catering to the social conventions of both the public and private spheres. Leigh Hunt's *Essays* from 1841 provide an example of the role that liqueurs such as those produced by Brizard played at this time. Commenting on how coffee was once drunk solo, Hunt observed that it had come to be 'taken as a digester, right upon that meal or

Johannes De Kuyper and Zoon's Parfait Amour, post-1973. Many companies started producing – and continue to produce – this popular liqueur with the whimsical name of 'Perfect Love'.

the wine, and sometimes does not even close it; or the digester itself is digested by a liquor of some sort called a *Chasse-Café* [coffee-chaser]. In the late 1800s, this 'coffee-chaser' morphed into a layered, primarily liqueur-based cocktail known as a Pousse-Café.

Art Nouveau advertising poster for Marie Brizard & Roger by the 'father of the modern advertising poster', Leonetto Cappiello, 1912. With his use of unconventional colours and dark backgrounds, Cappiello made images pop.

From Cultural Revolution
to Gastronomic Evolution

If Marie Antoinette had offered glasses of Parfait Amour to the angry mob instead of flippantly suggesting they 'eat cake' (or brioche, as the original French goes), perhaps she would have avoided an unwelcome tête-à-tête with Madame la Guillotine. Of course, modern historians now think that those words were never uttered by Louis XVI's queen consort, Marie-Antoinette-Josèphe-Jeanne d'Autriche-Lorraine. Still, with a baroque name like that, it is no wonder she was out of touch with the needs of anyone outside her rarefied circle.

Hyperbole aside, the French Revolution not only upended France's ancien regime, but sent the country's liqueur industry into a tailspin, just when it was starting to gain steam – not that it occurred without reason. While the First Estate (clergy) and the Second Estate (nobility) had money to burn, the Third Estate – comprised of the poor, the merchants and the middle class – struggled to make ends meet. Wine, tobacco, sugar, salt – all of them were taxed. These monetary inequities combined with emerging Enlightenment ideas, and the success of the American Revolution led to the Third Estate's protests.

When the Parisian masses stormed the Bastille on 14 July 1789, they were spitting mad, and the fervour spread like wildfire. Monasteries, including those that produced liqueurs, were closed; social settings – libraries, cafés, gardens – were ransacked. On every level, society was turned inside out. Revolution gave way to evolution, politically and socially, allowing France to redefine itself as a country and a people. It also created a power vacuum, which allowed for the emergence of one of the era's most influential figures, Napoleon Bonaparte.

Having risen to prominence amid the bloodshed, *le petit caporal* (the little corporal), as the army called him, became

First Consul of France in 1799. By 1804, he would declare himself emperor. While Napoleon's penchant for power has led many historians to label him a tyrant, he also helped to eradicate feudalism and to formalize laws with the Napoleonic Code. Likewise, the Napoleonic Wars stimulated the French economy, helping lay the groundwork for a productive France.

Napoleon was still an officer in the army when the Revolution erupted. Nonetheless, he supported the cause, even when French statesman Maximilien Robespierre orchestrated the Reign of Terror, during which thousands of nobles were executed. With the monarchy in tatters and the last vestiges of aristocratic life extinguished, the privileged few who were not executed quickly fled France, leaving their servants without jobs. A tenuous situation in the short run set the stage for the gastronomic – and bibulous – revolution to come.

Prior to the French Revolution, food had long been served in taverns and the like, but it was generally simple fare. Several

Les Trois Frères Provençaux was one of the most popular restaurants in Paris during the 1800s. Liqueurs would have been *de rigueur* on the menu.

specific turning points, pre- and post-Revolution, contributed to the expansion of food and drink venues. In 1765 a Parisian gentleman by the name of Monsieur Boulanger had opened what is considered to be the first restaurant. Unlike a café, which focused on drinks, Boulanger's establishment served 'restorative' broths for one's health. With Boulanger's broth, the stage was set for France's future restaurant culture.

In the wake of revolution, the culling of the aristocracy left French servants without jobs. The now-unemployed cooks and wait staff of the privileged class would soon reinvent themselves in the first fine-dining restaurants. The servant class was not the only one affected. By 1803 guilds, such as those for artisans like butchers or bakers, were banned. Having existed since the Middle Ages, these groups were seen by many as one of the last vestiges of the feudal system. With the eradication of the guilds and the transformation of the servant class, the door was opened to competition and a free market economy, both of which inspired people to open their own businesses.

Meanwhile, industrial advances shortened the workday for many citizens and encouraged the emergence of new classes – from professionals to merchants to factory workers. The underclass, of course, still existed and struggled to make ends meet, but the growing middle class had time and money. Leisure time (and a full wallet) soon equated to pleasure time; with the desire for pleasure and community, more varied locales arose to fill the need.

In the early 1800s, Paris alone was host to more than 3,000 restaurants, as well as hundreds of cafés and bistros, which sold food and drink. As the nineteenth century dawned, food as an art form became à la mode; its epicentre was Paris. The *Almanach des gourmandes* (Food Lover's Almanac) of 1803 recorded this transformation, noting that 'gastronomy became the fashion of the day.' Many of the emerging cookbooks appealed to and were sometimes written by the new class of professional chefs. Antoine B. Beauvilliers, who had been chef to King Louis XVIII, wrote the first cookbook focused on fine French cuisine. Notably, it included multiple liqueur recipes.

In the first volume of *Civilization and Capitalism, 15th–18th Century* (1979), Fernand Braudel observed of distilled alcohol, 'The sixteenth century created it; the seventeenth century consolidated it; the eighteenth popularized it.' Revolution opened the door to a burgeoning new social structure, which would continue to expand in the nineteenth century. This, coupled with industrial advancements and an evolution in dining, offered a rich opportunity for *liqueuristes* to peddle their wares. More importantly, the quality, cost and availability of these alcoholic delights slowly allowed liqueur to take its place in society as a social lubricant, not just a medicinal panacea.

Advertising poster for Liqueur Menthe-Pastille by Ferdinand
Misti-Mifliez, *c.* 1900.

4
Invention, Industry and Commercialization: Drinking in Post-Revolutionary France

Real G-g-green Chartreuse . . .
There are five distinct tastes
as it trickles over the tongue.
It is like swallowing a sp-spectrum.

Anthony Blanche in Evelyn Waugh, *Brideshead Revisited* (1945)

Just as the French Revolution opened the door to gastronomy, the Industrial Revolution had profound effects on the commercial expansion and production methods of liqueurs in France during the 1800s. Britain had been first out of the gate in terms of industry, which evolved from 1760 to 1830. By the 1840s, with the French Revolution very much in the rear-view mirror, France could capitalize on the industrial advances of the era. Among those most important to liqueur production were the cultivation of sugar beet and the refinement of the column still.

As one of liqueur's defining ingredients, sugar – its availability and its quality – had a direct effect on liqueur production. Colonization had led to the establishment of sugar cane plantations across the Caribbean and Brazil. Indeed, Brazil's sugar

Beta vulgaris altissima, the sugar beet. Unlike the round, deep reddish-purple or yellow beet used in cooking, the sugar beet is elongated and off-white in colour.

production had become so prolific by the mid-seventeenth century that the precious commodity could be regularly exported to Europe, where it was snapped up with unbridled enthusiasm. However, starting in 1790, sugar production screeched to a halt when slaves on what is now the island of Haiti revolted against French colonial control; the French West Indies had supplied 70 per cent of French sugar up to this point. By 1792 the situation was so bleak that protests erupted across Paris. The supply issues reached a peak across Europe during the Napoleonic Wars (1803–15), when Britain blockaded trade routes to the West Indies, leaving the continent without an easy sugar fix. Once again, sugar prices skyrocketed, if one could even find the crystalline grains for purchase.

Shrewdly, Napoleon recognized that people being unable to satisfy their sweet tooth would breed discontent, and he quickly focused on solving the problem, even going so far as to offer a monetary prize for the discovery of a cane sugar substitute. The answer would be found in a specific type of beet. Back in 1747, a Prussian chemist named Andreas Marggraf had managed to extract sucrose from sugar beets, showing that the sucrose structure was identical to that of sugarcane crystals. Marggraf's student Franz Karl Achard then developed an efficient – and cost-effective – method for extracting the sucrose; in 1801 he opened the first sugar beet factory in the Central European region of Silesia.

After French scientists presented Napoleon with loaves of beet sugar, the emperor was so impressed with the quality that he ordered that 32,000 hectares (79,000 acres) of sugar beets be planted. Within a few years, multitudes of commercial sugar beet factories sprang up across Europe from France to the Netherlands to Prussia. The demand for sugar continued, thus encouraging sugar beet cultivation and the ongoing development of sweeter varietals.

The end of the Napoleonic Wars and the subsequent dropping of the blockades made cane sugar available again, thus briefly putting a dent in beet sugar production. Despite the short-lived downturn in production, sugar beet commerce continued to expand, establishing a healthy foothold in Europe by 1850. The first sugar beet factory in the United States would arrive a few decades later, in 1870; by the early twentieth century, the American sugar beet industry posed strong competition to the European system. The liqueur industry at large started to discover that the sucrose supplied by sugar beet had multiple advantages. First, beet sugar was cheaper to produce. Second, unlike sugar cane, which required a tropical or subtropical climate, the sugar beet flourished in temperate zones, including

Northern Europe. This fact made it more easily obtainable and less expensive in terms of import and export. And, finally, beet sugar offered a milder flavour profile that did not interfere with or mask a liqueur's character. Today, numerous liqueur companies still use beet sugar as the sweetening agent in their products.

Sugar beet also had a somewhat concomitant link to the evolution of distilling because it became not only a reasonably priced source of sugar, but a convenient distilling ingredient for industrial alcohol. Indeed, an interest in producing sugar from sugar beet is what led Frenchman Jean-Baptiste Cellier-Blumenthal to design (in 1808) and patent (in 1813) the first continuous still for practical use. Various inventors, particularly Scotsman Robert Stein, improved on the effectiveness of Cellier-Blumenthal's design, but the name best remembered here is that of Aeneas Coffey.

The first sugar beet factory, Silesia, 1802.

In 1830 Coffey introduced a highly efficient still that could continuously produce alcohol 24 hours a day, seven days a week. With the Coffey still, distillers could now engage in uninterrupted production, resulting in a more economical and therefore more commercially viable product. Further, the cleaner, smoother base spirit, a product of the continuous distilling method, allowed for more enjoyable drinking. Even more importantly where liqueur is concerned, a clean spirit allowed truer flavours – fruits, nuts, spices and the like – to shine through. Prior to this more elegant base spirit, adulterations in the alcohol could both stop down and adulterate the liqueur's (or any spirit's) intended flavour.

Definitive Gallic Liqueurs

With the continuous still and plentiful sugar beet existing hand-in-glove, so to speak, liqueur was on the road to becoming more nuanced, more affordable and more plentiful. Indeed, a cursory look at the new liqueurs – and the emerging brands – that arrived in the nineteenth century shows a massive escalation in production. Even before Catherine de' Medici brought her distillers to court, the French already had a strong, albeit less sophisticated, distilling foundation in cordial production, whether prophylactic in nature or indigenous to a region.

A number of generic styles and proprietary brands are incontrovertibly linked to the Gallic nation. France's famed Chartreuse and Bénédictine share a medicinal past, originating within monastic orders whose members sourced herbal ingredients from the lush countryside around their monasteries. As monasteries were early pharmacopeias, the monks often served as apothecaries, producing herbal elixirs that, in several cases, evolved into modern liqueurs.

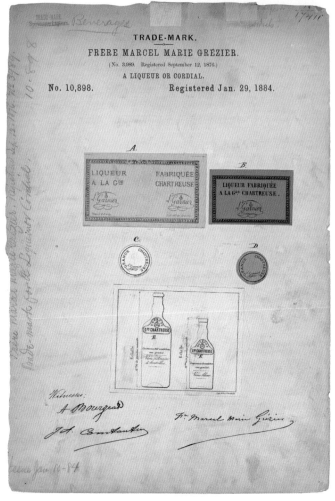

Trademark registration for Chartreuse, 'a liqueur or cordial', dated 1884.

The birth of Chartreuse liqueur can be traced back to 1257, the year that the Carthusian order founded a monastery in Vauvert. There, on the outskirts of Paris, the monks became acquainted with Arnaldus de Villanova and his student Raymond Lull, whose alchemical 'water of life' inspired the monks to create their own elixir. The definitive recipe for the 'Élixir Végétal de la Grande Chartreuse' was finally produced at the Grande Chartreuse monastery near Grenoble; its creation is documented in a 1764 manuscript entitled *Composition de l'Élixir de Chartreuse*. This high-ABV medicinal tonic, which the monks there still produce today, would become the base for the classic Chartreuse liqueur, whose vibrant green-yellow tone lends its name to the colour. A sweeter Chartreuse *jaune* (yellow) would be produced beginning in 1840; in 1852 the brand was finally trademarked.

In a history similar to Chartreuse, Bénédictine had its genesis with a monastic order in 1510 at the Abbey of Fécamp in Normandy, France. In 1863 a gentleman named Alexander Le Grande bottled a recipe that had been given to him by Fécamp's last surviving monk. In honour of the order, Le Grande dubbed the liqueur Bénédictine and used the term *D.O.M*, *Deo optimo maximo*, meaning, 'To God most good, most great,' as a token of respect.

While the above herbal elixirs are two of the most emblematic liqueurs of France, two other specific French categories – crème liqueurs and the orange-flavoured triple sec – have had a definitive influence on liqueur production in general. Not to be confused with cream liqueurs, crème liqueurs do not, in fact, contain cream or any dairy whatsoever. Rather, the 'crème' in the name refers to the spirit's texture. In contrast to a standard liqueur, crème liqueurs contain more sugar, resulting in a thicker, more luscious feel in the mouth. As defined by European Economic Community standards, liqueurs must have 100 grams (3½ oz) of sugar per litre. (In the United States, it is at least 2.5 per cent sugar.) In contrast, the standard crème style has 200 grams (7 oz).

Among the most representative examples of this style are crème de cassis and crème de menthe. Dijon-based liqueuriste Auguste-Denis Lagoute created the first commercial recipe for crème de cassis in 1841, using the distinctive cassis berries (known generically as blackcurrants) that proliferated in the region. While cassis liqueur can be made elsewhere, the specific nomenclature 'Crème de Cassis de Dijon' identifies a liqueur that uses only berries sourced in Dijon.

Some decades later, in 1885, chemist Émile Giffard created his Menthe-Pastille, having been inspired by his colleague Jean-Pierre-Joseph d'Arcet's restorative mint lozenge known as Pastille Vichy. Crème de menthe is produced in both clear, or 'white', and green styles. Despite sharing the same minty flavour, each style serves a different purpose, primarily related to colour with the saturated green style lending the defining tone to mint-green cocktails such as the Grasshopper (crème de menthe, crème de cacao and double (heavy) cream).

Along with crème liqueurs, the French made their own mark in the orange liqueur category. While the region of Flanders, as well as the Dutch, can lay claim to the earliest curaçaos, the French took a different approach in their creation of triple sec. Whereas orange curaçao uses brandy and is made in a pot still, triple sec is the exact opposite. Its usual column distillation method produces a clear – and cleaner – spirit. Also, triple sec tends to be higher proof and employ less sugar than the curaçao style, presenting a drier, less sweet profile.

This 'dryness' is part of what gives triple sec its 'dry' designation. The phrase 'triple sec' literally translates as 'triple dry'. Semantically speaking, some claim that it also might have originally meant 'triple distilled'. This is a credible idea since *sec* in French means both 'dry' as an adjective and, when describing a

Cointreau advertising poster, 1930s, by Charles Loupot. Loupot was tasked with updating the old-fashioned look of 'Pierrot Cointreau', a version of the popular commedia dell'arte clown designed by artist Nicolas Tamagno in 1898, for a new version more in keeping with the Art Deco aesthetic of the 1930s.

production method, 'distilled'. As for the 'triple' descriptor, it has been suggested by turns as referring either to the dryness or a multiple distillation method, as well as to the possible use of three types of oranges (or simply clever marketing).

Combier lays claim to the invention of the first triple sec in 1834, while the ubiquitous Cointreau followed in 1849. Then, in 1891, Louis-Alexandre Marnier created his eponymous Grand Marnier for the Café Royal in London, where orange liqueur had become all the rage. With its cognac base and amber tone, Grand Marnier is essentially a curaçao/triple sec hybrid.

Historically, France produced multitudes of other liqueurs, many of which are now obsolete. Others such as those above still exist and retain an authoritative place in the French liqueur lexicon.

Commercialization and Codification

With the continued emergence of commercial liqueur brands in France (as well as in other countries), the need to codify liqueurs – and, to a greater degree, clearly define the various proper methods of distillation in general – was more essential than ever before. It was one thing for the lady of the house or the local tradesman to distil their own cordials; it was quite another for commercial distilling houses to consistently produce and distribute liqueurs on a large, consistent, lucrative scale for public consumption.

Signalling a change in how liqueurs were perceived, one can compare John French's 1651 *Art of Distillation* with Pierre Duplais' *A Treatise on the Manufacture and Distillation of Alcoholic Liquors*. French's instruction manual or recipe book was little more than a concise handbook of fifty or so pages, with frequent references to alchemy, as well as recipes that had specific medicinal applications. In contrast, Duplais offered over five hundred pages of detailed instructions, definitions and codifications. Indeed, the section devoted solely to liqueurs is roughly the same length as French's entire book.

The second part of Duplais' *Treatise* focuses specifically on the 'Distillation of Perfumed Waters, Liqueurs, Essences, etc.' It covers everything from aromatic waters and tinctures to volatile oils and essences, each of which serves a distinct purpose. Likewise, he devotes around fifty pages to the intricacies of sugar, including its use in syrups. Of sugar, he specifically states that 'sugar, suitable for the use of the liquoriste, is obtained exclusively from cane and beets.' Further, he points out that these sugars are 'absolutely identical, and do not differ one from the other when refined to the same degree of purity'.

While Duplais states that either beet or cane sugar can be used with the same result, he stresses that the overall quality of the liqueur can still differ based on various parameters. Duplais defined these parameters to an exacting degree, noting that 'the classification of liqueurs depends on the proportions of alcohol, perfume, sugar and water employed in the manufacture, as well as in the care given to their preparation.'

Duplais' system of 'grading' starts with the lowest quality, *ordinaire* (common), progresses to *demi-fine* (half-fine) and *fine* (fine), with the premiere level being *surfine* (super fine). To identify these levels, Duplais recommends using a saccharometer, an essential tool invented by Scottish chemist Thomas Thomson, which allowed the distiller to estimate the gravity in liquids containing sugar. In the specific case of liqueurs, the saccharometer allowed for the measurement of the cordial's density, which is established by its sugar content. Such measurements become crucial not only when trying to maintain consistency between batches, but when certifying that the specific liqueur being made falls within its designated parameters.

Likewise, amounts of sugar and water vary. As the quality of the liqueur increases, so too does the amount of sugar. From *ordinaire* to *surfine*, the amount more than doubles. Conversely, the amount of water that cuts the alcohol decreases as the quality level rises. All of this is to say that the more ordinary liqueurs are lower in strength and sweetness, while the finer levels increase in strength and sweetness, as well as general quality of ingredients.

Names of liqueurs also provided a clue as to their quality levels. Liqueurs *ordinaires* generally use the terms *huile* (oil) or *eau* (water), as in Eau de Noyau or Huile de Roses. *Surfine* styles go by the terms 'crèmes' and 'elixirs'. Providing a glimpse into the range of liqueurs being produced and made available at the time, Duplais further categorizes *surfine* liqueurs as 'française, etrangères et des îles' (French, foreign and West Indian). He makes particular mention of fruit- or aromatic- infused ratafias, which still enjoyed popularity in the nineteenth century.

Today, many liqueurs possess straightforward names that simply describe their contents – crème de cassis, anisette, maraschino – or are long-established brands such as Chartreuse and Cointreau. In Duplais' day, the selection was far more seductive and ephemeral, as the author notes here:

> As for the names peculiar to each liqueur, the variety is infinite, and we cannot pretend to indicate all of them; moreover, the originality and eccentricity of some names, such as *esprit de Chateaubriand, d'Abd-el-Kadir, de Napoleon, liqueur de la polka, de la Couronne*, no matter what, &c., proves that they have nothing serious or fixed in them, but are only a matter of fancy; a new and highly colored label and a different tint transform almost any known liqueur into something new.

There was clearly concern regarding ersatz products, as Duplais devotes time to instruct his reader on how to recognize 'fraudulent' liqueurs. While numerous other distilling manuals appeared during this era, the *Treatise* remains the unofficial bible for liqueur production. Whether or not Duplais realized what a seminal work his manual would become, his contribution was immense, particularly in an era when people were ready and able to embrace recreation and leisure time.

During the post-Revolutionary period and throughout the nineteenth century, France would continue to distinguish herself in the liqueur world with an almost urgent dedication and undeniable skill. From the blood of 1789 sprang new economies and invigorated industry, which coalesced to make commercial spirits production faster, easier and more cost efficient. Massive socio-political upheaval restructured society and affected how people could spend their time. As European ways of eating and drinking evolved in cafés, restaurants and at home, products rose to fill the need. Liqueur had finally attained a specifically convivial role as what Braudel terms an 'accessible luxury'. While the quality and cost varied, liqueurs were available to and consumed by almost everyone.

As in France, other countries developed their own burgeoning commercial liqueur industries, but none was more influenced by France than Italy. Similar to the French concept of *joie de vivre*, the Italian idea of *la dolce vita* came to symbolize a breezy, relaxed way of life. While these countries are the most illustrative of this lifestyle, many other countries across Europe embrace similarly languid social rhythms and daily rituals – meeting friends at a café, enjoying a before-dinner drink, lingering over a long meal. These rituals are deeply intertwined with a class of liqueurs specifically meant to be consumed before and after meals. These liqueurs, all of them featuring a crucial and often intense bitter component, are so much a part of the European milieu that they command their own distinctive category.

5
Bitter Pleasures

Bad digestion is the root of all evil.
Hippocrates

The effects of the French Revolution washed across Europe in almost relentless waves as the oppressed classes gained the courage to stand up for equality. Many countries began to reshape themselves, powered by new social structures and stronger economies, which were in turn aided by advances in science and industry. However, as much of Northern Europe moved forward, the people of Italy struggled to find direction.

During the Middle Ages, Italy's location on the Mediterranean had allowed it to dominate trade and establish powerful infrastructure that influenced all of Europe. The region's access to Eastern knowledge had resulted in Italian alchemists creating the first Western liqueurs, as well as ushering in the Humanistic school of thought. However, these momentous contributions stemmed primarily from sovereign realms including the northern republics of Florence and Venice, as well as Rome and Naples in the middle and south of the peninsula, respectively. The country at large was still divided, and much of it, the south in particular, remained agrarian. This left a mottled collection of regions with no central government, at the mercy of capricious

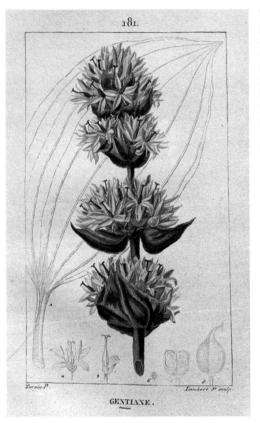

The herb gentian. Amarogentin, which is responsible for gentian's bitterness, is one of the most bitter compounds found in nature.

European countries (primarily the French, and the Austrian and Spanish Habsburgs) who were clamouring for territory. These power struggles led to the Italian Wars (1494–1559), during which Italy was carved into a patchwork of kingdoms, duchies and republics, each with its own, often foreign, hegemony.

In the midst of this explosive period, Martin Luther's *Ninety-Five Theses* (1517) attacked the corruption of the Catholic Church and inspired the Protestant Reformation. The Roman Catholic Church fought back viciously with its own Counter-

Reformation, leading all of Europe to take sides politically and religiously in the European Wars of Religion. To further control dissent, the Church declared Humanism to be heretical. Many of the great minds of the Italian Renaissance, including Galileo, were labelled heretics and excommunicated.

To complicate matters, Italy's once-prized Mediterranean location had hampered its involvement in the Age of Discovery, which had taken place mainly on the Atlantic. While countless Italian explorers such as Columbus and Vespucci discovered new continents, they sailed under the banners of other countries. By 1600 Italy's economy, which had ruled supreme during the Renaissance, was in shambles, and its populace faced uncertainty on all fronts. In its divided state and lack of hegemony, Italy as a whole benefited little from the post-Renaissance Scientific Revolution and the Humanism-driven Enlightenment thinking it inspired. In this environment, mass market liqueur had little chance to establish a foothold. Indeed, by the late 1700s, both France and the Netherlands had laid claim to the commercial liqueur throne. Ironically, Italy, the birthplace of Western liqueur production, floundered in the shadow of its more unified and now-Enlightened neighbours.

All of that changed, albeit gradually, in the wake of the French Revolution. When Napoleon marched into and claimed Rome and northern Italy in 1779, his arrival was unwelcome to many. Yet he symbolically ignited the Italians' hunger for change, a hunger that had been quietly percolating for some time. It is worth noting that, while most histories use his French name of Napoleon Bonaparte, the future French emperor was born Napoleone di Buonaparte on the Genoese-controlled island of Corsica. You might say that, in some ways, he was more Italian than French.

Invoking the ideals of the French Revolution, Napoleon planted the seeds that grew into Italy's mid-nineteenth-century

Luxardo export catalogue displaying seven liqueurs in the company's range beyond their well-known maraschino.

opposite: Advertisement for Galliano, 1966. In the 1960s and '70s, the brand used the 'Fond of Things Italiano' slogan to embody the allure of Italian culture for American drinkers.

Fond of things Italiano?
Mix these drinks with Galliano.

Serve cocktails Italian style with Galliano, the legendary
liqueur "distilled from the rays of the sun".
For those with adventurous taste, may we suggest the following
prize winning recipes from around the world.

BOSSA NOVA SPECIAL
*(Prize Winning
Recipe-Nassau Beach
Hotel Competition, Bahamas)*
1 oz. Galliano
1 oz. Light Rum
¼ oz. Apricot Flavored Brandy
2 oz. Pineapple Juice
½ oz. White of Egg
¼ oz. Lemon Juice
*Shake well, pour into a
tall glass with ice cubes
and decorate with fruit.*

**ITALIAN
STINGER COCKTAIL**
1 oz. Galliano
1¼ oz. Brandy
*Shake well with cracked ice.
Strain into cocktail glass.*

GOLDEN CADILLAC
1 oz. Galliano
1 oz. White Creme de Cacao
1 oz. Cream
*Place in blender with small quantity of
crushed ice. Use low speed for short
time until creamy. Pour into champagne glass.*

GALLIANO MIST
Fill old-fashioned glass with
cracked ice. Pour 1 oz. Galliano
over ice and squeeze and drop
¼ section fresh lime into glass.
Stir and serve.

**GOLDEN
DREAM COCKTAIL**
*(Prize Winning Recipe—
United Kingdom
Bartenders Guild)*
1 oz. Galliano
½ oz. Cointreau
½ oz. Orange Juice
½ oz. Cream
*Shake in cracked ice.
Strain into cocktail glass.*

GAY GALLIANO
*(Prize Winning Recipe—
Sandy Lane Hotel, Barbados, W.I.)*
¾ oz. Galliano   1½ oz. Rum
½ Fresh lime juice
*Put ingredients into blender
with shaved ice. Mix until
thick (semi-frozen). Pour
into champagne glass and garnish
with twist of lime peel.*

MILANO
*(Prize Winning Recipe
Copenhagen, Denmark)*
1 part Gin
1 part Galliano
1 part fresh lime juice
*Shake with ice and strain into
cocktail glass. Serve with cherry.*

ITALIAN HEATHER
(Prize Winning Cocktail Milan, Italy)
1½ oz. Scotch   ½ oz. Galliano
*Stir with ice. Strain into glass
with twist of lemon peel.*

Risorgimento. Meaning 'resurgence' in English, the movement led to the unification of Italy. Gradually, Italy transformed from a melange of independent, feudal city-states into a single-minded entity prepared for the industrial future. Not surprisingly, Italy's foray into the commercial liqueur industry gained steam.

From the early years of the nineteenth century into the beginning of the twentieth, many sweet Italian liqueurs arrived on the scene. Luxardo stepped into the commercial liqueur world in 1821 with Luxardo Maraschino Originale, whose sour marasca cherry pits came from the city of Zara. Once the Venetian capital of Dalmatia, Zara is now part of modern Croatia and known as Zadar. By the 1830s the Luxardo company sold its liqueurs internationally, including to the United States, Cuba, China and Japan.

The Lazzaroni family claims to have invented the first amaretto in 1851, flavouring it with an infusion of their Amaretti del Chiostro di Saronno biscuits; the same year, Luigi Manzi created his digestive sambuca using green aniseed. Then, in 1860, Strega arrived. Based on a recipe for an ancient herbal cordial, the name, which means 'witch', was inspired by the local legends of witches' gatherings in Benevento, Campania. Towards the latter half of the century, in 1875, Nicola Pallini began making cordials, including anise, rosolio, vanilla, cinnamon, almond and limoncello. Today Pallini's limoncello and Romana Sambuca are both recognized brands. And, on the cusp of the twentieth century, both the herbal-vanilla Galliano (1896) and Amaretto di Saronno (early 1900s) came to fruition. Strega, Galliano and Saronno (today known as Disaronno), in particular, would reach commercial heights in the USA in the 1960s and '70s, where they were featured in multiple cocktails.

Along with these proprietary brands, many of the above liqueurs – limoncello, maraschino, sambuca – are generic styles, thus allowing multiple companies to offer their own versions. Likewise, small-scale cordial-making still survives across Italy's provinces, where distillers offer products with a particularly regional flair. From Venice's strawberry liqueur known as fragolino to the walnut nocino of Emilia-Romagna, these liqueurs are, in some ways, the truest expressions of Italian cordial making, born of local traditions and employing carefully guarded family recipes.

Prandial Protocols

The sweeter liqueurs like those mentioned above evolved to cater to people's love affair with sugar. However, a distinct subset of bitter liqueurs emerged, harkening back to and embracing liqueur's medicinal past. Early healers understood the benefits of bitter plants to treat stomach ailments: the medical importance of digestion traces its roots back to Hippocrates. His concept of humorism stressed balancing one's metabolism in order to maintain health. Even though Hippocrates' statement about the evils of bad digestion may be a tad dramatic, it indirectly inspired the evolution of the European bitter liqueurs that even today are sipped either before or after a meal.

With these spirits, bitterness is not only a defining characteristic, but an essential one, because bitter flavours activate the digestive system. Aperitifs/aperitivos, from the Latin *apero* (to open), are sipped before a meal in order to prime the appetite, while digestifs/digestivos, from the Latin *digestivus* (to be dissolved), arrive after the meal to help process one's food.

An even more specific classification for these liqueurs exists as well. Signifying the term 'bitter', the style is called *amaro* in Italy, *amer* in France and *halbbitter* in the Germanic regions. Both *amer* and *amaro* translate to mean 'bitter'; *halbbitter* simply means 'half bitter'. Ironically, while everyone inherently understands the concept of bitterness, not everyone will agree on what is, or is not, bitter. There is, in fact, no single definition of 'bitterness'. Dictionaries offer words such as 'acrid', 'astringent' and 'unpleasantly sharp', but these are vague descriptors. Both our genetics and our cultural food exposure affect our perception of bitterness, which helps explain why some cultures prefer sweeter foods, while others enjoy bitter flavours.

Regardless of our modern tolerance levels, our bodies are evolutionarily primed to react to bitterness because it often equates with danger. For instance, castor beans contain the deadly chemical ricin; fruit stones, like those historically used in ratafia, contain cyanide. However, studies in the last decade suggest that bitterness plays a more active role beyond simply being an early warning system, so to speak.

The moment a pungent flavour enters our mouths, bitter taste receptors, dubbed TAS2R and T2R, go to work. The sensation of bitterness activates the digestive system. First, the taste buds on the tongue produce saliva, which is a trigger to expel the toxin before it is eaten. Then, the stomach receptors produce gastric juices, which slow the process of digestion, keeping the toxin in the stomach longer, digesting it more fully and, hopefully, expelling it more efficiently.

Bitter liqueurs trigger these same poison detectors, but, in this case, the body's response has a salubrious effect on the general process of eating. Before a meal, saliva activates in anticipation of eating, thus priming the appetite. Likewise, the stomach's activity, which prolongs the digestive process, helps the body process its food more effectively.

Italy's Bitter Love Affair

From a boozy, archaeological standpoint, amaro is simply the great-great-grandchild of the herbal elixirs first created in Italian monasteries and pharmacopeiae. Classified as potable bitters, amari should not be confused with aromatic bitters such as the non-potable Angostura, which are used incrementally to flavour cocktails.

Amaro often challenges those trying to define it. Sother Teague, Beverage Director at New York's Amor y Amargo, the first dedicated bitters tasting room and bar in the United States, describes amari as 'terroir-driven drinks that are unique to each producer and region'. But this individuality comes with a price, according to Teague, 'because there are no real rules to define the category. Just three words really: bitter, sweet, liqueur.' Some amari use wine-based grappa (Italian pomace brandy) as a base alcohol, while others use neutral spirit. Depending on the base, the alcohol-by-volume (ABV) can range from around 15 per cent to a brawny 45 per cent or more. Further, each amaro employs a specific, and often wildly varied, combination of herbs, flowers, barks and spices, resulting in a panoply of sweet and bitter notes.

Beyond the monastic or pharmacological roots, amaro can trace its modern gestation to 1786 in the Piedmontese city of Turin. That year, Antonio Benedetto Carpano created the first vermouth, an aromatized, fortified wine that employs many of the same bitter botanicals that amari use. Carpano vermouth enthralled King Vittorio Amadeo III and led the city of Turin to become the centre of aperitivo culture. The popularity of this botanically infused vermouth set the stage for the popularity of the spirits-based bitter drinks that arrived in the 1800s.

It is no coincidence that the first vermouth hailed from Turin in the progressive Piedmont region of Italy. France had

Advertisement for Strega, 1902. The image embraces the brand's
supernatural legend of witches gathering walnuts by moonlight.

annexed Turin in 1802, influencing the area's social and commercial development. Not surprisingly, many of the earliest branded
Italian liqueurs, whether sweet or bitter, often evolved in areas
with more industrialized – and, as a result, more cosmopolitan
– cities. More advanced cities naturally offered more cultural
options, particularly caffès, which became one of the logical
spots to sip liqueurs. Following in the footsteps of Venice's Caffè
Florian (1720), caffès and the culture surrounding them grew
exponentially: Florence's Caffè Gilli (1733), Turin's Caffè Fiorio
(1780) and Baratti & Milano (1858), and Milan's Caffè Zucca
(1867) were but a few. Many enterprising producers even opened
their own caffès to showcase their amari. As in France, the
Italian caffè became a natural locale for lingering over a drink

while engaging in political and cultural debate. By the nineteenth century, many caffès morphed into bars. In Italy, 'BAR' was an acronym for *Banco a Ristoro*, or refreshment counter.

While some of the lower-ABV amari are consumed before a meal, generally with a splash of soda water or a twist of orange, the majority find their home as post-meal digestive aids. In fact, as in France, where an after-dinner drink was often referred to as a *chasse-café*, or coffee chaser, so too in Italy the digestif is called an *amazzacaffè*, a 'coffee killer', to be consumed after one's espresso.

The first spirit-based amaro, Ramazzotti, was created in 1815 by herbalist Ausano Ramazzotti. With a keen sense for business, Ramazzotti sold his amaro at his Milan caffè, where it garnered the cognoscenti's favour. The broad combination of herbs, spices, fruits and flowers – gentian, rhubarb, sweet orange peels, kola nut and cinchona – offers a textbook representation of what an amaro is all about: aromatic and bitter with a touch of sweetness.

Over the course of the century, creative distillers enthusiastically followed suit to highlight the botanicals of their specific region. As more amari came to market, the liqueurs often fell into distinct sub-categories, including alpine, *rabarbaro*, *carciofo*, red bitter and fernet. For example, Braulio (1875) is considered an alpine amaro because it hails from a mountain region and employs alpine herbs such as gentian. Rabarbaro Zucca (1915) is a prime example of the *rabarbaro* (rhubarb) style. And Cynar, which came late to the party in 1952, is emblematic of the *carciofo* (artichoke) variety, although artichokes are but one of many botanicals in this style.

The red bitter and fernet categories bear further mention because of their defining roles in drinks culture. The best-known red bitters – Campari (1860) and Aperol (1919) – share superstar status thanks to their respective contributions to the

Negroni (Campari, gin, sweet vermouth) and the breezy, bubbly Aperol Spritz (Aperol, soda water (club soda), prosecco), respectively. While both of these amari are orange-forward, Campari packs a sharp, medicinal punch, with 24 per cent ABV (in the USA, but 28 per cent for the rest of the world) compared to its gentler, 11 per cent ABV counterpart. Logically, red bitters are so named because of their vibrant red-orange colour. Historically, the cochineal beetle gave these liqueurs their carmine tone, but today alternative colouring is generally used.

Fernet, whose best-known brand is Fernet-Branca (1845), is distinctive because people rarely realize it is a category, not a

Chromo-lithograph advertising card for Fernet-Branca, Dei Fili Branca, c. 1870–1900.

brand. With its muscular character, the fernet style is a complex symphony of flavours ranging from liquorice, to mint, to menthol. Regardless of the brand, these amari unapologetically march across the tongue in a full-on militaristic assault.

Despite its aggressive character or perhaps because of it, Fernet-Branca in particular enjoys a cult following around the world. Originally billing itself as a herbal treatment for cholera, amaro gained momentum in 1876 when an advert in the first edition of *Il Corriere della Sera* generated praise for the formula from medical professionals. Beyond its medicinal applications, Fernet-Branca played the defining role in the now-classic Hanky Panky cocktail. The Fernet-spiked sweet Martini variation was created in 1903 by Ada Coleman, the first female bartender at the American Bar in London's Savoy Hotel. Starting in 1907, the brand opened distilleries in Buenos Aires, New York, St Louis, Missouri, and Chiasso, Switzerland. In Italy, Fernet-Branca is often used to spike a cup of espresso, creating a *caffè corretto*. Halfway around the world in Argentina, where many inhabitants are of Italian ancestry, urban Argentinians created the 'Fernando', a long drink mixing Branca with cola. Today, in the bartending community, the cult amaro is convivially referred to as 'the bartender's handshake' because it is offered to colleagues as a show of hospitality.

Magic Hour

With the decades of French occupation in various regions of Italy, Italian and French social customs often melded to create a hybrid cultural aesthetic. Much as digestive amari function in Italy, aperitifs serve an almost-mystical role in French culture. 'On prend l'apéro,' says one Frenchman to another. Basically, it means 'Let's grab a drink,' specifically 'Let's grab an aperitif.'

Unlike the rather giddy tone of the American phrase 'Happy Hour', which bids goodbye to the workday, *l'apéro* greets the beginning of the evening and all of its mysteries. Sometimes the French do indeed drink aperitifs after work, but often they simply enjoy them before dinner or before a get-together with friends. The tradition is not about drinking, but socializing. In recent years, the concept of the *apéro dînatoire* (essentially a buffet-style dinner with aperitifs and cocktails) has gained traction in France.

Like amari, amers often contain a harmony of bitter notes. However, several botanicals in particular – gentian, cinchona and pine or pine-like ingredients – tend to crop up again and again. While marrying with whatever other flavouring elements they meet, these three distinctive botanicals offer the defining note in whatever liqueur they grace.

The bitterness present in gentian root comes from the chemical compound known as amarogentin, which is so bitter that it is used to scientifically measure bitterness. The genesis of the word dates back to the second century BCE. It takes its name from Gentius, the last king of Illyria, who used a gentian-based elixir to treat injuries in battle. Despite their similar names, the gentian plant should not be confused with gentian violet, a wholly synthetic dye that takes its name from the purple-based colour known as violet. In contrast, one of the more popular species used in liqueurs, *Gentian lutia*, is a vibrant yellow. To make the situation more confusing, gentian violet bears no relation to the violets used in crème de violette.

While gentian plays a complementary role in multiple Italian amari and many German bitters, it is the primary note in some of the most popular French amers. Of these, the first to arrive on the scene was Bonal Gentiane-Quina, in 1865. Bonal is sometimes classified specifically as a quinine-based aperitif because of the inclusion of 'quina' in the name. But gentian is just as essential (if not more central) to this amer's character. Emphasizing gentian's primary importance, the label clearly announces 'Gentiane à consumer très frais' (literally, 'Gentian to be consumed very fresh').

While arriving after Bonal in 1889, Suze is perhaps the most iconic amer, seducing the bitter-attuned French palate in relative short order. With its vibrant yellow colour and august columnar bottle, the brand was ubiquitous enough in French society that Picasso featured it in his 1912 Cubist collage entitled *Glass and Bottle of Suze*. Gentian-forward Salers, a combination of distillate and macerate, was introduced in 1885. A number of quinquina-based aperitifs, such as Dubonnet (1846) and Byrrh (1866) are actually aromatized wines, which are fortified with spirit and then flavoured with botanicals. While not liqueurs by definition, these two wines are often referred to, and even mistaken for, their boozier cousins, particularly because of their roles as aperitifs.

Along with gentian, quinquina defines an entire group of aperitifs. The term 'quinquina' is often used interchangeably with cinchona, quina and the most familiar quinine. Native to South America, the cinchona tree was used by the Indigenous peoples of Peru and surrounding regions. They introduced it to Spanish Jesuits in the 1600s; these missionaries took it back to Europe, where it was hailed as a medical miracle that could cure malaria.

In 1820 French researchers managed to isolate the quinine compound, which quickly became the de facto malaria prophylactic. In the following decades, quinine started to feature not only in tonic water, but in many bitter liqueurs. A Gallic mainstay to this day, Amer Picon was created in 1837 by French cavalry sergeant Gaétan Picon, who was stationed in mosquito-ridden Algeria. While the flavours of gentian and bitter orange are more pronounced, the quinquina helped deliver a much-needed dose of quinine to malaria-plagued soldiers, earning the bitter therapeutic the name 'African Amer'. Picon eventually became a favourite of Basque immigrants to America, who created the Picon Punch, a potent combination of Picon, brandy, grenadine and soda water.

Several conifer botanicals round out the jewels in the crown of French amer ingredients. The piney scents and

Pablo Picasso, *Glass and Bottle of Suze*, 1912, pasted papers, gouache and charcoal.

Colorado Distillery Golden Moon's Amer dit Picon is based on a famous old Amer formula from 1837. The company is in the process of rebranding the product as Amer Antik.

flavours apparent in this category call to mind a walk through an alpine forest, each reflecting the distinctive character of the conifer element from which they are sourced. Both Armand Guy's Vert Sapin and Deniset-Klainguer's Grande Liqueur de Sapins employ fir tree buds (*sapin* is French for 'fir'). Zirbenz Stone Pine Liqueur from Austria has a more resinous quality that comes from the young pinecones, called 'fruit', of the Arolla pine tree.

The après-ski liqueur génépy, or génépi, which is produced in multiple alpine regions, could be loosely included in this 'conifer' category, due to its somewhat similar pine-like flavour and aroma. The main botanical, however, is not a conifer, but rather a variety of artemisia (wormwood) called mountain sage.

The style has many variations, including centerbe liqueur from Italy. While génépy is characterized by its use of wormwood, it is not related to the wormwood-based absinthe, which is often incorrectly referred to as a liqueur. Absinthe has no added sugar, thus falling outside the liqueur category. (Absinthe's liquorice-forward cousins Pernod and Pastis fall somewhere between spirit and liqueur because of their low sugar content.)

By far the most esoteric style in the coniferous category is that of the now-defunct pine tar liqueurs. Known as *goudrons*, meaning 'tar' in French, these drinks trace their lineage back to medieval times. Tar as a panacea reached its apex in the floridly titled book *Siris: A Chain of Philosophical Reflexions and Inquiries Concerning the Virtues of Tar Water* (1744). Therein, Anglo-Irish Bishop George Berkeley extolled tar's medicinal benefits, exclaiming: 'Hail vulgar juice of never-fading pine! Cheap as thou art, thy virtues are divine.' Multiple producers jumped on the tar bandwagon, each touting the hygienic quality of their refreshing digestive cordials.

Arrivage d'un convoi de citrons d'Italie (1ᵉ choix)

A Bigallet & Jinot convoy carrying lemons from Italy. Note the word 'Goudrons' on the side of the wagon, *c.* 19th century.

Jägermeister advertisement, 1959: 'Germany's most drunk Halbbitter!'

Amari and amers, such as those above, are essentially living fossils of the liqueur world, as they so clearly trace their roots back to monastic medicines used for digestion and stomach troubles. However, starting in the 1800s, these herbal elixirs began to morph into cultural symbols – the *joie de vivre* of the

French, the *dolce vita* of the Italians. Fuelled by industrialization and continued social stratification, café and restaurant culture spread across Europe. Not surprisingly, the social role of aperitifs and digestifs grew, albeit not necessarily with the same ritualistic zeal as in France and Italy.

In the Netherlands, residents have been sipping Petrus Boonekamp liqueur since the 1700s, while Central and Eastern Europe developed halbbitters (half-bitters). Often called *Kräuterlikör* in German, Schwartzhog (1700) and Underberg (1846) are but two examples. Today perhaps the best-known brand is Jägermeister (1934), which has a cult following as enthusiastic as the one for Fernet-Branca. Unicum (1790) is the national drink of Hungary; the Czech Republic's Becherovka (1807) was originally marketed as 'English bitters' because the recipe was from an English doctor. Across the globe in Argentina, Amargo Obrero launched in 1887 as a working man's alternative to the sweet drinks of the rich.

These liqueurs and hundreds of others were truly the children of the revolution. Not only do they illustrate the feverish level of production of the nineteenth century in particular, but they became essential, even defining, companions to the European lifestyle. In contrast to the bitter-embracing palate of the Europeans, the congenital sweet tooth present in Britain and America often led those countries to embrace more sugary sippers.

Indeed, while continental Europe favoured its more prandial pleasures, the upper crust of English society preferred sweet, boozy punches in public, while polite British ladies surreptitiously swigged their equally sweet and boozy cordials in private. Further afield, the ever-on-the-move Americans slowly started to integrate liqueurs into what is arguably the most profound development in the history of spirits and the greatest boon to the world of liqueurs: the cocktail.

6

From the Flowing Bowl to the Cock-Tail

When e'en a bowl of punch we make,
Four striking opposites we take;
The strong, the small, the sharp, the sweet,
Together mix'd, most kindly meet;
And when they happily unite,
The bowl is pregnant with delight.
Oxford Night Caps (1827)

When this buoyant rhyme about punch graced the pages of *Oxford Night Caps* in 1827, the British had been guzzling the stuff for more than two hundred years. Brought back to England by sailors on the eastern routes, the earliest versions were rough and potent DIY tipples, nothing close to the delightfully pregnant bowl in the Victorian ditty above. Today, we often think of punch as the fruity, sugar-water drink gulped down at children's parties; however, it has a much more noble history. Indeed, the mix of strong, small, sharp and sweet is one of Britain's most important contributions to liqueur's future.

The history of punch itself is long and complicated. One possible etymology for the word 'punch' is that it is derived from the Sanskrit word *pañcāmṛta*, which combines the terms *pañca* (five) and *amṛta* (ambrosia). In his book *A Curious History of*

Food (2013), author Ian Crofton translates *pañcāmṛta* as the lyrical phrase 'five nectars of the gods'. A more truncated possibility is that the Hindi word for five, *panch* (derived from *pañcāmṛta*), conveniently refers to the five ingredients in the celebratory bowl: spirit, citrus, sugar, spice and water. But, since the number of punch ingredients can vary widely, this hypothesis does not quite ring true. Another possibility still is that the name stems from the term 'puncheon', a barrel that stored alcohol. Various other feasible derivations exist, demonstrating that punch's name is just as cloudy as its origins.

As for said origins, punch in some form very likely existed in the East long before any Europeans arrived there. The ingredients were readily available. Arrack, a strong spirit whose name simply means 'liquor', was distilled from a multitude of sources including the sap of coconut palm flowers in Ceylon, as well as sugar cane and red rice in Java. The latter version possesses a rum-like quality; it is known as Batavia arrack, from the Dutch name for the Indonesian capital (today Jakarta). Arrack, and then rum (both the English style and French *rhum agricole*) from the Caribbean, would become the boozy anchor in punch when it became popular first in England, then across Europe and, subsequently, in the American colonies.

Further, citrus, including lemons, limes and oranges, grew in abundance throughout South Asia, which was also ground zero for spices such as nutmeg and sugar. So, yes, perhaps the locals were guzzling their own version of the brew before the English arrived, but it is also probable that enterprising English sailors took the abundant ingredients and tossed them together to make an at least palatable, and hopefully pleasurable, drink. Had arrack not been available, aqua vitae would have done the trick. By the later 1500s ships were already being stocked with the 'water of life', whose lack of spoilage made it an attractive cargo, whether as a ration or a medicinal base.

William Hogarth, *A Midnight Modern Conversation*, 1733, print in red ink.

With these truths in mind, we can move forwards with the idea that English, and probably Dutch, sailors were merrily slugging punch in port and taking it or making it aboard ship by the end of the sixteenth century. The actual word 'punch', however, is not mentioned in print until 1623. That year, Robert Addams, an employee of the East India Company, wrote to a friend, wishing that the man 'keep good house . . . and drincke punch'. Fifteen years later, Johan Albert de Mandelslo, a German man working in India, recorded it as 'a kind of drink consisting of aqua vitae, rose-water, juice of citron and sugar'.

By the mid-1600s punch was served in English coffee-houses, where any man could gain entrance by paying a penny for a cup of coffee. Not coincidentally, these egalitarian coffee-houses became the prime meeting places for Enlightenment thinkers like Adam Smith and John Locke. Be it the boozy bliss, the promise of camaraderie or the chance to show off one's mixing prowess, punch seduced those who partook for a multitude of reasons. Over time, punch also became a symbol of both patriotism and status. The British Navy drank punch, and the British people loved their navy. Likewise, one could demonstrate one's wealth with punch because it not only required expensive ingredients like spices and citrus, but the free time to indulge in a bowl of booze. Charles Dickens himself was known for his punch-making skills. Indeed, punch and its promise of celebration were so dear to him that he owned a special nutmeg grater for just such occasions.

With its simple combination of sweet, sour, strong and weak, punch allowed for infinite creativity. In the nineteenth century, as ingredients and preparation became more sophisticated, liqueurs started finding their way into punches, acting as substitutes for or adjuncts to one or more of the main ingredients. Among these, curaçao is included in Royal Punch and plays a defining role in the aptly named Curaçao Punch; maraschino contributes its almond-like character to the Imperial and Garrick Club punches.

Beyond using standardized recipes, resourceful Victorian folk invented the 'fruit cup' or 'summer cup', essentially a punch-like drink that used gin as the base spirit. To this, people could add whatever liqueurs, fruits and spices they had on hand. Along with sloe gin, the fruit cup is one of England's most emblematic beverages, often enjoyed at picnics and sporting events. The term 'fruit cup' comes from the fact that it is generally served as a long drink, topped with lemonade, ginger ale or ginger beer and garnished with various fruits and the ubiquitous cucumber. In 1844 London oyster bar owner James Pimm created the first bottled version of the style at his Oyster Warehouse. The Pimm's Cup went on to become one of Britain's most favoured summer sippers.

By the 1840s punch had become a ready-to-drink consumable across Europe. In 1845 Cederlund's Caloric Punsch

Kronan Swedish Punsch, a modern iteration of the original style from Haus Alpenz.

from Sweden rose to fame. Generically, it was often referred to just as Caloric or Arrack Punsch. In the 12 May 1846 issue of the *London Daily News*, the pre-bottled and pre-mixed Vicker's Curaçao Punch was announced as 'stand[ing] pre-eminent as a finished specimen of what Punch should be'. A few decades later, William Terrington's *Cooling Cups and Dainty Drinks* (1869) offered multiple liqueur-enhanced 'cup' recipes that call for maraschino, curaçao, noyau and Chartreuse.

Aside from Pimm's and sloe gin, the British did not play a central role in liqueur production at this time. Instead, they favoured fine, foreign liqueurs such as those described above.

As stated in Mew and Ashton's 1892 *Drinks of the World*, 'The English have attained as yet no high rank as liqueur manufacturers.' The authors go on to mention that the liqueur industry is 'chiefly continental', noting Holland for its curaçao, Russia for kümmel and France for a multitude of spirits. In stark contrast, English cordials and cups, whether produced professionally or in the home, tended to be less exotic, almost homespun in their simplicity. It is worth noting that, in Britain, the term 'cordial' started to mean a sweetened, non-alcoholic drink or syrup, probably around the time that Rose's Lime Cordial (a lime/sugar syrup) was released.

Despite the fact that Britain had yet to distinguish itself in the production of major proprietary or brand-driven liqueurs, the country made a much more valuable contribution: the art of combining spirits, liqueurs and other modifiers like citrus in their punches and cups. These quintessentially British creations can be thought of as proto-cocktails, which laid the foundation for an entirely new breed of mixed drink. The British actually receive the credit for the first printed use of the word 'cocktail' – in the 20 March 1798 edition of London's *Morning Post and Gazetteer*. However, it is the Americans who made the drink what it is today, spreading the cocktail gospel around the globe and, in the process, giving liqueur a happy home. But before that could happen, America endured a lot of boozy growing pains.

America the Boozy-ful

From the start, alcohol was an essential part of life in Colonial America. Beer, wine, cider and spirits all played a role; people drank a lot and drank often. According to W. J. Rorabaugh in his tellingly titled *The Alcoholic Republic: An American Tradition* (1979), 'Americans between 1790 and 1830 drank more alcoholic beverages per capita than ever before or since.' Consumption spread across all of society, regardless of race, religion or sex.

Men were the greatest consumers of alcohol, usually straight spirits. As for cordials and liqueurs, they were, by and large, the domain of ladies. As in England, Americans perceived women as virtuous, delicate creatures, certainly not enthusiastic consumers of straight spirits. In public, however, it was accepted that a lady might need to partake of a 'medicinal' elixir, if her constitution was faltering. At home, 'fashionable people owned ornate liquor cases or elaborate sideboards that contained numerous bottles of various cordials, including mild, sweet, fruit-flavoured elixirs for the ladies,' as noted by Rorabaugh.

A number of events in the early 1800s influenced the future of liqueurs, albeit indirectly. America's first railroad, the

Baltimore and Ohio, arrived in 1827, setting the stage for easy transport of goods and people. That same year, the country's first fine dining restaurant – Delmonico's in New York – opened its doors, offering wealthy Americans the chance to emulate their aristocratic European cousins in high style. Over the century, fortunes were made and lost as a result of rapid industrialization and the boom-or-bust economy it engendered. A wealthier middle and an elite upper class emerged, eventually inspiring the term 'Gilded Age'. It was a time of enormous prosperity and indulgence for those who could afford it. As exemplars of an elegant life, liqueurs and cordials featured prominently during this time.

Newspaper accounts suggest that liqueurs were not only relatively easy to come by, but very much sought after. For example, an advertisement run by spirits merchant Thomas McMullen in the 24 December 1851 issue of New York's *Evening Post* states that the company sent its liqueurs 'with care to the remotest parts of the country'; during the same period, advertisements for cordials and liqueurs demonstrate that cities as disparate as Frankfort, Kentucky, and Honolulu, Hawaii, had access to liqueurs.

As the century wore on, the custom of drinking liqueurs gained traction with the younger crowd, as seen in an article dated 6 August 1888 in the *Los Angeles Daily Herald*. In response to the author's query, 'Have the liqueurs and cordials of Europe come into use to any extent over here?', a bartender is quoted as saying,

> The rising generation drink more for the excitement or sociability of the thing than from habit, and the stiff and occasional whiskey 'brace up' of their fathers is too potent a tipple when an evening out requires that the elbow shall be crooked frequently, or perhaps multiple times. Hence,

the adoption of various liqueurs taken in small but exhilarating sups, which in their cumulative potency lead to a weaving way, but less quickly and with less overpowering and stupefying effects than old-time John Barleycorn.

The article continues with a comment from a senior member of a local wholesaling house, who confirms, 'Yes, it is now considered the correct thing to top off dinner with cordials, or liqueurs,' both at home and in hotels and restaurants. Among the most popular liqueurs were Chartreuse and Bénédictine, while maraschino and curaçao were traditionally served to 'afternoon and evening callers'. Anisette, apparently, was 'a distinctly feminine beverage', as it 'leaves no taint on the breath, and the flush it produces is easily mistaken for rouge'.

While this new generation enjoyed after-dinner 'sups', much like their European cousins, they were simultaneously partaking in a concoction that would change the future of liqueur in all its many forms.

How the 'Cock-Tail' Changed Everything

In 1874 an American gentleman staying in London wrote to his wife and requested that she 'be sure to have in the bathroom, when I arrive, a bottle of Scotch whiskey, a lemon, some crushed sugar and a bottle of Angostura bitters'. That man was Mark Twain; his ingredient list was for a 'so-called cock-tail', which he enjoyed 'before breakfast, before dinner, and just before going to bed'. According to his letter, his digestion had never been better since he started enjoying this popular drink.

The original Cock-Tail – capital 'C' very much intended – was not a class of drinks, but a single, specific drink, generally prescribed medicinally. (Later, the word dropped the hyphen and became 'cocktail', at which point it became a catch-all phrase for all mixed alcoholic drinks.) Today, we know the Cock-Tail as the Old Fashioned (for all intents, a mixed-in-the-glass liqueur) and, while we no longer consume it for health, it still makes us feel pretty darn good. One of the drink's essential ingredients, as Twain pointed out, was bitters, a non-potable tincture of alcohol and various herbs or roots and so on, such as gentian and wormwood. Not to be confused with bitter amari, non-potable bitters still used many of the same ingredients as amari and for the same digestive purpose.

At this time, professional medicinal treatments remained somewhat primitive and were mistrusted by many, despite advances in both physiology and technology. Further, much of the care for illness was still provided at home by wives or mothers. Thus bitters became a trusted remedy for many ailments. The first modern aromatic bitters was created by London apothecary Richard Stoughton in 1712. Recipes for the brand appeared in various books, and the product was exported to America, where Boston distillers soon started making their own versions. Stoughton's disappeared in the 1800s, but Angostura bitters, created in 1824 by German army surgeon Johann Siegert, took its place. In 1832 apothecary Antoine Peychaud launched his eponymous brand in New Orleans. Both of these brands are essential ingredients in many classic cocktails, including Angostura in the Martinez and Peychaud's in the Vieux Carré. Not coincidentally, both of these cocktails contain liqueurs, maraschino in the former and Bénédictine in the latter.

In the late nineteenth century, there was a huge uptick in patent medicines, which were proprietary formulas with protected recipes. Taking advantage of the popularity of these cures, quack doctors, also called snake oil salesmen, often peddled ersatz goods that promised to do everything from growing one's hair to helping with kidney troubles. Even liqueurs themselves were part of the medicinal carousel; both crème de menthe and kümmel were common treatments for stomach issues.

Given the provincial state of medicine at this time, it is easy to see how the original Cock-Tail served as 'medicine'. Two of its primary ingredients – alcohol and sugar – had been used in prophylactic cordials since ancient times, while the third, bitters, now had a reputation as a healthful remedy. In addition to the Cock-Tail, liqueur-accented drinks were consumed by sporting gents after an indulgent night out. These morning-after concoctions included the Slow and Quick (gin with sloe gin) and the Pick-Me-Up (Angostura bitters, maraschino, Chartreuse and brandy).

In the early days of the Republic, Americans had enjoyed communal drinking around a spirited bowl of punch, much as their British peers did. This sort of recreation faded as daily life in the newly born United States of America became more demanding. America was now a go-go-go country; one simply did not have the time to idle away the hours in pursuit of bibulous convivialities. And so people discarded the punch bowl in favour of the cocktail glass, its individual delivery both efficient and customizable. If punch was essentially the first 'mixed' drink, then the American Cocktail (which would come to define an entire class of drinks) was the first *single-serving* mixed drink.

In 1862 the Cocktail and other mixed alcoholic drinks like those above appeared in *The Bar Tenders Guide: How to Mix Drinks; or, The Bon-Vivant's Companion* by Jerry Thomas. Thomas was quite the impresario, slinging drinks in premiere bars across the country and commanding a salary of $100 a week (equal to approximately $3,000 today). As the first drinks recipe book published in the English language, Thomas's work standardized recipes that are still in use today. Many of the cocktail recipes included liqueurs, which demonstrates that liqueurs were an essential part of the bartender's arsenal and, by

COSACK & CO BUFFALO

The vibrant illustrations on 1800s advertising cards like this one for Burdock
Blood Bitters captured the imagination. The stomach and blood 'remedy' was
one of many Quack-type tonics that used familiar medicinal herbs, but produced
doubtful results.

Postcard for the Hiram Walker Distillery in Peoria, Illinois, 1930–50.

extension, were in demand by the public. Additionally, Thomas also wrote a comprehensive 'How to' guide as an appendix to a manual by Christian Schultz, with recipes for 23 cordials, 20 ratafias, 16 liqueurs and 22 crèmes.

Curaçao was something of a go-to workhorse in the early cocktail days. It was used in both the brandy and gin Cocktails, as well as the Knickerbocker (rum, curaçao, raspberry syrup, lime juice) and multiple punches such as the Regent's and Roman. Along with curaçao, a few other liqueurs are called for specifically, including Chartreuse, kirschwasser and maraschino. In the 'Fancy Drinks' section of his book, Thomas offers four recipes for the layered, liqueur-dominant Pousse-Café. Down the line, these layered drinks would provide the architecture for the sweet shooters of the 1980s and '90s.

In the decades following Thomas's, cocktail recipe books flourished, and liqueurs continued to play a vital role in turn-of-the-century cocktails. In the ensuing decades, the market would be flooded with cocktail books, which frequently included recipes for making liqueurs. However, the days of needing to whip up an in-house batch of noyau or maraschino would soon end. Gradually, commercial American brands started to emerge, offering their own line-ups of European-style cordials. In the United States, Frenchman Charles Jacquin opened his company in 1884; Charles Jacquin et Cie. is the oldest cordials producer in the country.

In 1858 American-born Hiram Walker had established his eponymous distillery in Canada in order to avoid the challenges of the growing United States temperance movement. While best known at the time for its Canadian Club whiskey, the brand would go on to produce one of the largest lines of liqueurs in the world. In the post-Prohibition years, Hiram Walker implemented plans to build the largest distillery in the world (taking up 9 hectares, or 22 acres) in Peoria, Illinois, at the cost of $5 million. Walker was an innovator as well. Among his contributions, he was one of the first liquor producers to put actual labels on his bottles. Establishing what the company referred to as 'an American institution on American soil' set the stage for a strong U.S. presence that continues today despite many changes in ownership.

All Forbidden Joys

Americans drank whiskey (not to be confused with its more celebrated Scottish cousin whisky) in the 1800s with as much enthusiasm as the English drank gin in the 1700s. To say it was a popular tipple would do it a disservice. To say it was frequently a bit rough around the edges would be kind. Still, America loved its whiskey, whether corn-based bourbon or rye. Not surprisingly, two of the country's best-known liqueurs are whiskey-based, and both of them arrived in the 1800s. In 1874 a New Orleans bartender named Martin Wilkes Heron created

Forbidden Fruit liqueur is clearly featured on the Café des Beaux Arts menu.

a drink called Cuffs and Buttons. In 1889 Heron patented and bottled his creation with the slogans 'None Genuine But Mine' and 'Two per customer. No Gentleman would ask for more.' That drink would come to be known as Southern Comfort, a whiskey-forward liqueur accented by stone fruits and spices.

In 1884 the Hochstadter's brand, in association with the Charles Jacquin Company, had started producing a bottled version of the popular rock-candy-sweetened rye whiskey being sold in saloons across the country. After Prohibition, Hochstadter's and Jacquin merged into America's first liqueur company as Charles Jacquin et Cie., Inc. in 1934. While the brand's Rock & Rye disappeared for many decades, the recipe on which it was based inspired a modern version called Slow and Low. Released to the public in 2013 by the Cooper Spirits Company and created by late founder Robert Cooper, grandson of Jacquin's original president, the Slow and Low is, for all intents, an Old Fashioned in a bottle. Despite this bottled cocktail's whopping 84 proof, its ingredients – a combination of spirit, rock candy and honey, as well as Angostura bitters and orange peel – firmly places it in the liqueur camp. In 2016, the company released a ready-to-drink, tinned version of the product.

Aside from these whiskey-based styles, the majority of cordials produced in America at this time were generic versions of popular liqueurs like crème de menthe, sloe gin or maraschino. Then, in 1902 Basque brothers Louis, André and Jacques Bustanoby opened the posh Café des Beaux Arts in New York City, where they introduced the grapefruit-flavoured Forbidden Fruit. The deep orange-red liqueur seduced the female clientele, who congregated in the Ladies Bar, a spot specifically for women to enjoy a drink with one another without the need of an escort or the condemnation of the society pages.

With its come-hither name and distinctive bottle design – clearly resembling a royal orb – Forbidden Fruit aptly demonstrated the marketing acumen of the Bustanoby boys. The liqueur quickly became all the rage among the the high society types. In the 29 April 1905 edition of *Brooklyn Life*, a section titled 'Fads and Fashion' noted that the cordial was so popular that the young ladies of New York had a standing joke about how 'the band of filigree like an equator notifies the lady who keeps it for nips in her boudoir that the contents are half gone.'

Pre-1964 bottle of Forbidden Fruit. Note the 'crown' cap and filigree band adding a regal quality to the bottle.

The Bustanoby brothers soon started advertising their liqueur commercially; its fame spread to the UK, where the *Café Royale Cocktail Book* (1930) required it for a number of drinks. In 1937 the Jacquin company acquired the rights to the cordial but would stop production in the 1970s in order to repurpose the bottle for their new raspberry liqueur Chambord. To date, only one company – Lee Spirits – has attempted to recreate the elusive grapefruit liqueur, producing their own version based on copious research.

Teetotallers Unite

Since the Colonies were founded and even before, the place of alcohol in society, for both nourishment and succour, had been debated. In 1673 Increase Mather, a Puritan clergyman in the

Massachusetts Bay Colony, had stated that 'Drink is in itself a creature of God and to be received with thankfulness.' But, as drunkenness became a national pastime, temperance societies begged to disagree, and this opposition only gained steam in the ensuing centuries.

In the 1800s temperance groups – from America to Australia, the United Kingdom to Ukraine – actively fought what they saw as the evils of alcohol; liqueur did not escape criticism. Of all the temperance movements, America was very much at the centre. In fact, judgement was widespread enough that a rather scathing article appeared in New York's *The Sun* newspaper on 21 December 1885. The propriety of Mr Frye, the restaurant keeper of the U.S. Senate, was called into question, as he had included 'nine fiery liqueurs' on the Senate wine list. Of these liqueurs – including maraschino, curaçao, kümmel and anisette – one of the senators questionably defended their inclusion by stating that they fell under the purview of wine- or malt-based spirits.

While the late 1800s to around 1910 were a true Golden Age of the Cocktail, that glorious era was swiftly snuffed out when the teetotallers got their way. The spectre of American Prohibition arrived in 1919. The next year, the Volstead Act took effect, banning the production and sale of consumable alcohol. Like all spirits, liqueurs – and the mixed drinks that featured them – suffered. Not surprisingly, like a petulant child, when the government said 'No, you won't,' the people simply said 'Yes, we will.' And they promptly proceeded to break every rule that the Eighteenth Amendment enshrined, from boozing it up in illicit speakeasies to heading overseas (England, France, Cuba) where they could freely partake in their favourite cocktails.

7
Twentieth-Century Blues

Tender young things, who have just been taken off stick candy,
prefer complicated pink and creamy drinks which satisfy their
beastly appetite for sweets and at the same time offer an agreeable
sense of sinfulness.

Extract from *Shake 'Em Up!* cocktail book (1930)

The 1980s were the height of overly sweet, liqueur-centric
cocktails with often crudely (and intentionally) seductive
names. A shining example of how liqueurs defined these cocktails is the Slow Screw family of drinks. The original version
simply adds one liqueur – sloe gin – to the standard Screwdriver, a relatively insipid long drink of vodka and orange
juice. Adding Galliano produces a Slow Screw Up Against
the Wall; the 'wall' references the Harvey Wallbanger cocktail
of the 1950s, '60s and '70s. But let's not stop there. Southern
Comfort makes it 'Comfortable'. And, if you want a Slow
Comfortable Fuzzy Screw Up Against the Wall, you'll find
your answer in a bit of sweet, syrupy peach schnapps (from
the Fuzzy Navel). In the 1980s, liqueurs were cocktail super-
stars. And while it took more than half a century for drinks
such as the Slow Screw to enter the bartending lexicon, the
long journey to get there began in the post-Prohibition years,

Molinari Sambuca advertisement, *c.* 1971. Sambuca brands like Antica, Luxardo and Meletti, each of which use centuries-old recipes, still produce bottlings today.

when a series of seemingly unrelated events carried cocktails into an age of excess.

A Vacation in a Glass

Having weathered the dry years of Prohibition and still faced with the spectre of the Great Depression, Americans were primed for a party once the 1930s rolled around. Right after Prohibition was repealed, a young gentleman named Ernest Raymond Beaumont Gantt, also known as Donn Beach, opened Don the Beachcomber in Hollywood; the exoticism of the

South Pacific combined with potent, Caribbean-style rum drinks seduced movie stars and anyone else who could afford it (despite the 90-minute wait). In creating this Polynesian paradise, Beach can be considered the founding father of the tiki craze, which led to an entire 'backyard Polynesia' lifestyle in the following decades. But Beach should not get all the credit.

The allure of the tropics and its rum-based tipples had been established long before Prohibition. In 1866 the Sacramento Union had published Mark Twain's *Letters from Hawaii*, exposing the curious public to the lush island paradise. When the Hawaiian Islands collectively become a U.S. territory in 1898, mainland America was captivated by the island culture, particularly the music with its defining ukelele/steel-guitar twang. On a separate island front, United Fruit, a Jamaican company that supplied bananas to North America and England, started offering passage to the island of Jamaica for American tourists in 1899. Demand for accommodation led to the establishment of

With their boozy-fruity profiles, cocktails like Don the Beachcomber's Zombie and other tiki drinks primed people's palates for the sweeter cocktails of the 1960s, '70s and '80s.

the Titchfield and Myrtle Bank hotels, where guests were seduced by the simultaneously simple and elegant Planter's Punch (rum, lime juice, simple syrup).

By the early 1900s Americans would head to Cuba regularly, where they got a taste of what was destined to be a future classic – the daiquiri. Essentially a tweaked Planter's Punch, the cocktail had been invented in 1896 by Jennings Stockton Cox Jr, who worked for John D. Rockefeller in the town of Daiquiri, Cuba. The cocktail eventually found its way to Havana, where Prohibition-weary Americans sought boozy solace.

In Havana, drinkers made a beeline for El Floridita bar, where *cantinero* ('bartender' in Spanish) Constante Ribalaigua held court. Constante created multiple versions of the basic daiquiri by adding liqueurs as the defining modifiers: the No. 2 used curaçao and the No. 3 employed maraschino, while the No. 4 featured curaçao and the surprising addition of white crème de cacao. Despite its simplicity, the daiquiri captured everything tiki culture would come to symbolize. As Jeff Berry notes in *Potions of the Caribbean* (2013), the daiquiri was 'exotic, musical, romantic. The word would become the clarion call of the next army to storm Cuba: the middle-class American tourist.'

With visions of the tropics dancing in his head, Beach opened his Polynesian getaway to capture the same magic people had experienced on their Caribbean escapes. With the Planter's Punch triumvirate of rum, lime and sugar, Beach's concoctions blended booze, fruit juices and a myriad of liqueurs that called to mind distant locales. Whether the liqueur was the spice-forward falernum (sometimes rum-based, sometimes nonalcoholic), the allspice-based pimento dram or Don's own proprietary Gardenia Mix (a combination of honey, cinnamon, vanilla and allspice dram), these liqueur-enhanced cocktails were a holiday in a glass. As he was known for saying, 'If you can't get to paradise, I'll bring it to you.'

Ironically, 'tiki' immediately conjures images of Polynesia, despite the fact that the main cocktail ingredient is rum, a product of the Caribbean. Beach's reason for emphasizing the South Pacific was clever. The Caribbean – with its convenient location, sultry weather and multitude of islands to choose from – was literally in America's backyard; in contrast, Polynesia was isolated in the middle of the South Pacific, the embodiment of distant, inaccessible, unadulterated exoticism. A year after Beach opened his locale, Victor Bergeron launched Trader Vic's in Oakland, offering many of the same or similar drinks at his establishment. Soon imitators spread across the country, and tiki drinks appeared on menus everywhere.

The tiki craze was not only here to stay, but its sweet, fruity cocktails primed the American palate for the turbo-sweet drinks of later decades. Perhaps more importantly, tiki created a theatricality that elicited delighted 'oohs' and 'ahs' from the customers. Huge punch bowls, often served alight with sparks or flames, catered to giddy groups. Abundant fruity, floral garnishes decking pseudo-Polynesian-themed glassware reinforced the 'drinking can be fun' vibe, a theme that would explode in the 1960s, '70s and '80s. After all, no one can frown when served a cocktail with an umbrella.

Liqueur as Social Microscope

We have seen time and time again how booze responds to social change, acting as something of a cultural barometer. The tiki trend was only one harbinger of the liqueur-based party drinks to come in later decades. Numerous other factors helped set in motion the plethora of creamy, slushy, sugary concoctions that would come to rule supreme. The reasons are many, but among them is the essential idea of liberation.

While buying a drink was illegal during Prohibition, this did not stop the Jazz Babies from indulging in covert cocktail parties. Of these wild events, the 'Topics of the Times' column in the 27 June 1922 issue of the *New York Times* lamented the au courant use of the word 'party'. Said the *Times*, a party was 'a gathering of persons who can have a "good time" only when highly stimulated by strong waters, always, in these days, illicitly acquired'. Books such as Robert Vermiere's *Cocktails, How to Make Them* (1922) and *Shake 'Em Up* (1930) supplied recipes for at-home shindigs; manuals like these would continue in the following decades, exposing eager amateur mixologists to the world of drink-making.

Further afield, in London, the posh, bohemian set partied their privileged lives away, leading the press to dub them the Bright Young Things; their antics were roundly parodied by Evelyn Waugh in his 1930 book *Vile Bodies*. The hedonism of the youth culture thumbed its nose at convention and knocked elbows with equally young and hedonistic American expats such as F. Scott Fitzgerald. Both in Europe and the United States, the post-war Jazz Age set in motion a series of disparate events that helped build the road towards the liqueur-based (often artificially flavoured) drink styles of the later twentieth century.

During Prohibition, commercial sour mix had started to show up in bars and for home use, presaging the artificial-tasting, 'instant', powdered versions of the 1970s and '80s. The invention of the electric blender in 1922 would make possible the slushy, liqueur-based 'milkshakes' of the future. And, while vodka had been made in Russia possibly dating back to the ninth century, the first vodka in America was not available until 1934. While it took a few decades to catch on, this flavourless, colourless spirit would fully capture the public's fascination by the 1950s. Its appeal was logical. It still provided a boozy kick but did not leave any trace of alcohol on your breath – it left you 'breathless', as Smirnoff's 1958 campaign announced. More importantly, when it came to cocktails, vodka had no defining taste as whiskey or gin did. Not only did it offer a blank canvas for other flavours, but it demanded them, as it had none of its own. It would become the perfect foil for the liqueur- and juice-powered cocktails of later decades.

Beyond any of the above tangible advances, the most influential social change came in the form of liberation. During the Jazz Age, the youth culture, especially women, strayed from convention. The flapper movement championed the rights of all women to express themselves freely, flaunting their femininity, sexuality and power. This sexual revolution would affect America and, to some extent, Europe for generations, eventually exploding in the 1960s and continuing in the 1970s. Perhaps tangentially, but important nonetheless, these movements established women as an essential component in the economy. Their purchasing power, taste palate and general attitudes would have a lasting effect on drinks culture, something that the Bustanoby brothers had intuited with their Ladies Bar and the launch of Forbidden Fruit.

Leading up to and during the Second World War, liqueurs helped define many new cocktails. Tequila drinks arrived in the United States, showing up in the Cointreau-accented margarita and the El Diablo, which uses cassis, ginger beer and lime. Providing a future base for the Slow Screw family of drinks, the vodka-orange juice Screwdriver was created as well. And, along with tiki's continued popularity, sweet-and-creamy, liqueur-defined 'milkshakes' such as the Grasshopper (crème de menthe), Alexander (crème de cacao) and the new kid in the family, the Pink Squirrel (noyau and cacao), catered to society's boozy sweet spot.

At this point, it is clear that a gradual shift in cocktail profiles, from the more serious, spirit-driven styles to those with a

Kahlúa and its fellow coffee liqueurs are essential for numerous cocktails, including the Black Russian, the White Russian and the Espresso Martini.

fruitier, sweeter formula, had begun. Since their inception, classic cocktails accented by liqueurs had always possessed a level of sweetness, but it was a subtle hint. Indeed, recipe books in the pre- and post-Prohibition eras show liqueurs generally being used in conservative amounts – a dash, a drop, a teaspoon – even in tiki drinks.

In the following decades, liqueurs would come to be seen less as modifiers and more as defining ingredients. Case in point: the Black Russian. Introduced at the Brussels Hotel Metropole in 1949, it combined a roughly two-to-one ratio of vodka to the coffee-based Kahlúa liqueur, which had launched in the 1930s. The Vodka Stinger, a variation on the classic brandy-based version, was composed of equal parts vodka and crème de menthe. And, capitalizing again on island allure, in 1957 the

Bols company tasked the Hilton Hawaiian Village's bartender Harry Yee to create a cocktail with the company's blue curaçao. The Blue Hawaii – blue curacao, pineapple juice, vodka and rum – rode the wave of the continuing tiki trend and provided something of a road map for the Day-Glo cocktails of the 1970s.

How Sweet It Is

In a 12 December 2012 article for *Saveur* magazine, cocktail and spirits writer Robert Simonson identified the 1970s as the 'Death Valley' of cocktails. Simonson's summation of this decade – 'a time of sloppy, foolish drinks made with sour mix and other risible shortcuts to flavour and christened with foolish monikers like Mudslide and Freddie Fudpucker' – might be unkind, but, from a certain perspective, it is quite true. Despite the lack of finesse in drinks culture, the 1970s were unequivocally unapologetic about their penchant for sugar-amped cocktails, layered shooters and boozy milkshakes.

In 1960s America, the youth culture had been far more interested in transformative experiences. Instead of sipping cocktails, which they saw as 'square', many of them favoured psychedelics and other drugs. But come the 1970s, many of the hippies of the '60s were settling into suburbia and embracing all of its accoutrements. Quite often, sugar became the new 'drug' of choice. Unfortunately, during this decade, a combination of issues – global politics, climate, production and consumption – turned sugar cost and availability upside down, eventually affecting the quality of many liqueurs.

In the 1970s, as world sugar prices skyrocketed, high fructose corn syrup (HFCS) stepped in to save the day. Invented in 1957, this liquid combination of fructose and glucose would come to be used in a vast array of consumables from baked goods to drinks. While HFCS and sucrose (cane and beet sugars) possess relatively similar levels of sweetness, HFCS appealed to manufacturers because it was cheap to produce, easy to use and readily available. For these reasons, many larger, cost-conscious liqueur companies switched to using HFCS in their products. While this may all seem to have a secondary relationship to liqueur's evolution, it casts a light on the emerging trend – particularly in the enormous American market – towards sweet and cheap products.

Additionally, artificial flavours and colours, far less expensive than their natural counterparts, became the norm in many products. Artificial colours – the blue in blue curaçao or the green in crème de menthe – are generally brighter, cheaper and longer lasting than natural ones. Likewise, artificial flavours cut costs, easily mimicking (although rarely equalling) natural flavours. Completing the ersatz combination of sweeteners, flavours and colours was the popularity of bottled sour mix. Commercial sour mixes had been used since Prohibition and continued to gain popularity in the following decades. Whether bottled or later powdered, these massively inferior mashups combined citrus juices (often artificial versions thereof), corn syrup, artificial colours and preservatives. The odds were, if you ordered a sweet drink in the 1970s, you would be slurping down a lot of artificial ingredients.

The sugary concoctions of this era had a number of things in common. They often used orange juice, bottled or tinned. If the drink called for a spirit, it was probably vodka. If the drink called for liqueur, it was, by turn, syrupy sweet, cream-based and/or brightly coloured, creating drinks more fit for a sweet-shop than a bar. As for cocktail names, they varied from tame, tropical, escapist monikers such as the Blue Lagoon to the blatantly come-hither Sex on the Beach. The trippy, free love era had thumbed its nose at old-fashioned cocktail culture, but it was hard to say no to the new breed of downright decadent concoctions that emerged during this time.

Two emblematic brands of this era beautifully illustrate the range of flavours and styles with which people fell in love. The 1973 invention of Baileys Irish Cream was particularly important to the development of modern liqueurs, as it was the first true cream liqueur. Featuring two of Ireland's iconic products – dairy cream and Irish whiskey – Baileys was sold primarily in the UK and exported mainly to the Netherlands and Australia at first. Kismet struck when Baileys managed to get into the duty-free shops at UK airports. Soon enough, American tourists started taking the liqueur home; some time after, a United States distribution deal was struck.

As the name suggests, cream liqueurs contain cream. In order to produce a shelf-stable product, the liqueur goes through the process of homogenization, which emulsifies the fat in the milk. Not only does this prevent the cream from separating, but the emulsion also retards spoilage because it contains enough

Baileys coffee/teacups from the 1990s.

Amarula, which came to market in 1989, is just one of many modern iterations of the cream liqueur style. The brand is known for its philanthropic efforts to save African bush elephants, which show a predilection for the marula fruit.

alcohol to stop microbial growth. In the ensuing decades up to the present, Baileys has inspired numerous other cream liqueur brands including other Irish creams, as well as Disaronno Velvet, RumChata (capturing the cinnamon-vanilla flavour of Mexico's horchata) and the South African Amarula, with indigenous marula fruit.

Equally sweet, but favouring juicy fruit over sweet cream, was Midori, based on muskmelon. Originally launched by Suntory in Japan under the name Hermes Melon Liqueur, the brand sported the catchier and simpler 'Midori' (meaning green in Japanese) moniker when it arrived in the United

'You can build a whole party around Harvey,' instructs Galliano's *Discover Gold* recipe booklet (1972).

States in 1978. Debuting at Studio 54 during a cast party for the recently released *Saturday Night Fever*, the neon-green colour of Midori in the brand's Japanese Gin and Tonic completed the kaleidoscopic disco vibe.

Along with new brands came new cocktails such as Midori's Gin and Tonic riff and the go-to party shooter the B-52, a shot glass layered with Baileys, coffee liqueur and orange liqueur. Familiar names such as Galliano offered their own sought-after drinks. As one of the most requested brands in the bell-bottom decade, Galliano was the key ingredient in the Golden Cadillac, with crème de cacao and cream, as well as the infamous Harvey Wallbanger. Truly representative of the era's drinks, the Wallbanger was an easy-sipping combination of vodka, orange juice and Galliano that capitalized on the surfing subculture of the time with its mellow surfer dude character named Harvey.

Amaretto created its calling card with the Amaretto Sour and the Alabama Slammer, the latter of whose familiar ingredients – sloe gin, amaretto and Southern Comfort – had been around far longer than Midori or Baileys. Said to have emerged at or near a university in Alabama, the Slammer recipe first appeared in print in the 1971 *Playboy Bartender's Guide*. The chuggable drink gained further traction when American chain restaurant T.G.I. Friday's started serving it by the pitcher, which essentially made it a convenient, pourable, modern punch.

With drinks such as the Harvey Wallbanger being advertised in Galliano's *Discover Gold* recipe pamphlet and easy-to-make shots such as the B-52 at the fore, the cocktails that emerged in the 1970s eschewed propriety and promised a good time. In fact, while this era is often condemned for its backwards motion regarding cocktail evolution, it evolved in its own unique ways. Instead of being perceived as uptight and formal, they were just fun. At-home cocktail gatherings became so ingrained in the culture that many American homes featured cocktail trolleys

In 1982, Charles Jacquin et Cie., Inc. appropriated the Forbidden Fruit bottle to use for their new Chambord liqueur. In 2010, a more streamlined bottle style – without the crown cap and gold ornamentation – would be introduced.

and wet bars. Some industrious folks even converted their basements or rec rooms into freestanding bars, replete with rotating vinyl bar stools, a full workspace and display shelves for popular liqueurs of the day.

To satisfy the in-home bar culture, *Jones' Complete Bar Guide* by bartender Stan Jones was released in 1977. The comprehensive book included more than 4,000 cocktail recipes, old and new. Not one page could be turned without some liqueur being called for, whether generic, such as maraschino and crème de menthe, or proprietary, such as Crème d'Yvette or Forbidden Fruit. In the following decades, many of these liqueurs faded into obscurity until the cocktail renaissance of the twenty-first century resurrected them.

Just as Jones's book had done for the 1970s, the 1988 movie *Cocktail* offered a glimpse into the drinks of the '80s. Holding court at the bar one evening, swaggering bartender Brian

Flanagan, played by Tom Cruise, calls himself the 'Last Barman Poet'. He boisterously lists some of his 'sweet and snazzy' drinks such as the Three-Toed Sloth (sloe gin, apple schnapps, dark rum) and the Orgasm (Baileys Irish Cream, Kahlúa, amaretto, cream). One of the key products he touts is 'the schnapps made of peach'. He is talking about John DeKuyper & Sons' Original Peachtree Schnapps, which caught fire soon after its release in 1984. Not to be confused with traditional German schnapps, which contains no added sugar, an American-style schnapps like Peachtree is a sweet cordial. The man behind the recipe, National Distillers flavour scientist Earl LaRoe, likely had no idea what a ruckus he would cause when he created the liqueur. Indeed, Peachtree inaugurated an entirely new 'peach schnapps' liqueur category. It also defined some of the most popular drinks of the era, including the perennially popular Fuzzy Navel (peach schnapps, orange juice). Peachtree sold 13 million bottles in its first ten months; today, Japan is the brand's largest market.

The Orgasm and the Fuzzy Navel are illustrative of a truly 1980s drink trend: sex. Neon colours and fruity flavours definitely caught people's eye, but if there was one thing that sold a drink better than anything else, it was innuendo. Cocktails with lurid names provided some of the worst (or, perhaps, best) pick-up-lines ever. Liqueurs added the yummy factor. There was the Screaming Orgasm (vodka, amaretto, Kahlúa, Baileys) and the Slippery Nipple (sambuca, Baileys Irish Cream), the Sex on the Beach (Fuzzy Navel with vodka and cranberry juice and sometimes black raspberry liqueur) and the already dissected Slow Screw (sloe gin, gin or vodka, orange juice), which begat an entire tribe of frisky, liqueur-forward children.

Whereas the classic cocktails of the Golden Age employed measured doses of liqueurs, the drinks of the 1960s, '70s and '80s used liqueurs with an almost reckless, gleeful abandon and often in proportions that eclipsed any other flavours. The philosophy was that if one liqueur was good, then why not two, three or even four? If orange juice or vodka were in play, all the better. If you could turn it into a milkshake or a shot, do it!

These were the decades that sent liqueurs, and how they were used, into somewhat retrograde motion. Their role was no longer as a polite after-dinner drink or an accent in a cocktail. Instead, they were front and centre, starting and fuelling the party, and they did a bang-up job of it. However, fruity, frothy, sex-in-a-glass descriptors would soon exchange adjectives with cocktails that were sophisticated, subtle and, once again, classy. It would take another decade to see this coalesce, but the wheels were already turning. The days of sour mix, bottled juice and liqueur-upon-liqueur layers would soon give way to the 1990s, the decade when the 'cocktail renaissance' quietly, very quietly, began.

Created by Doug Ankrah in London in 2002, the Pornstar Martini – made with vanilla, vodka, the French liqueur Passoã, passion fruit juice and lime – continues to be a perennial favourite in bars around the world, partly because of the lascivious name, but mostly because of the luscious flavour.

8

The New Golden Age

When evening quickens in the street, comes a pause in the day's
occupation that is known as the cocktail hour.
Bernard DeVoto, *The Hour: A Cocktail Manifesto* (1951)

The 2000s would usher in a new age of cocktail culture when
classic recipes, ingredients and techniques were rediscovered.
However, before this era of enormous change could begin, bartenders, customers and the drinks that brought them together
would have to go through some serious growing pains. Entering
the 1990s, liqueurs were still little more than a delivery system
for a childlike sugar rush. But, as the decade progressed, the
Mudslides and Slippery Nipples found at the neighbourhood
'flair' restaurant grew up, albeit in a very bastardized way. These
new drinks were still very sweet, but they assumed the form of
the most classic of all adult beverages: the Martini.

'Tini Culture

In the cocktail pantheon, the combination of gin and vermouth
will always be regarded as the traditional Martini. But from the
1950s onwards, gin faced stiff competition from vodka. In large

part due to Smirnoff's breathless advertising campaign, as well as the fact that 'the sexiest man alive', James Bond, favoured the spirit, the Vodka Martini became the standard.

But the Vodka Martinis of the 1990s would have left James Bond gobsmacked. Vermouth and bitters were out, and the blank, alcoholic canvas provided by vodka was one on which fruit juices and often-syrupy liqueurs could shine. This new Martini was Bond's drink in name only. Anything poured into a classic V-shaped glass and mixed with vodka was called a Martini, even if it was little more than last decade's shooter. What was most important was not what you were drinking, but the way you looked – and felt – when you drank it. Socialites liked the sex appeal of the drinks. Suburbanites enjoyed being sophisticated like their big city friends. The craze gave birth to chichi 'Martini' menus, often peddling ten or more dessert-like cocktails with liqueurs enjoying star status and vodka taking a backseat. As long as you looked suave and mysterious hoisting your cool, V-shaped glass, did the cloying chocolate-raspberry concoction inside really matter?

During this era, several liqueur flavours took centre stage and almost singlehandedly drove the 1990s Martini craze. One of the most popular was apple; the most emblematic example was Sour Apple Pucker. DeKuyper USA had already dazzled with Peachtree in the 1980s, providing a flavour barometer of the time. Similarly, Sour Apple Pucker's candy profile perfectly captured the zeitgeist of the '90s 'tini mindset; the liqueur's release in 1996 is indelibly linked to a cocktail created that same year at Lola's in Los Angeles.

The Appletini was a product of practicality. Lola's restaurant owner Loren Dunsworth wanted to use up some extra vodka and apple schnapps. Bartender Adam Karsten combined them, naming the drink the Adam's Apple Martini. The rest is 'tini history. It took a while for the recipe to reach the aptly named Big Apple, but the now-generic Appletini hit pay dirt in a *New York Times* story dated 4 October 2000. The *Times* announced the arrival of 'a crisp, new cocktail made from vodka and some variety of apple spirit' (meaning liqueur) and conclusively stated, 'The apple martini is officially in season.'

The popularity of the Appletini would soon be shared by the Cosmopolitan and the Espresso Martini. The Cosmo is essentially a Kamikaze – vodka, triple sec, lime juice – with a splash of cranberry. In 1988 at New York's Odeon, bartender Toby Cecchini created what is now the accepted recipe, using Absolut Citron (one of the new, flavoured, but not sweetened, vodkas hitting the market), plus Cointreau, lime juice and cranberry juice. The Cointreau does take a back seat to the cranberry, but the drink would not be a Cosmo without it.

As for the Espresso Martini, the original version was created by the profoundly influential London bartender Dick Bradsell in the early 1980s. At that time, it was a simple combination of vodka and espresso dubbed the Vodka Espresso. In 1997, when Bradsell started bartending at London's popular bar Match, he kept pace with the 'tini scene. He anointed his soon-to-be trendy cocktail the Espresso Martini.

With their easy-drinking flavours and sophisticated appearance, sweet Martinis accomplished a vital task: they showed this generation that cocktails could be cool again. But, for a purist, this new perception begged the question: how can a couple of ounces of sweetly amped-up liquid possibly be called a Martini? Does the glass make the drink or do the ingredients?

From the Kitchen to the Bar

Part of the move towards classic cocktails that used liqueurs in a more subtle manner happened because of the changes in modern food culture. Much as MTV did with music and pop culture in the 1980s, the 1993 establishment of the Food Network exposed the average consumer to new cuisines, cooking techniques and ingredients. These, in turn, fostered curiosity and encouraged people to explore the culinary world.

American restaurants started to serve 'hybrid' cuisines, offering a cross-pollination of flavours from locales as varied as France, Japan and Latin America. The farm-to-table movement, which had quietly started in 1971 with Alice Waters's Chez Panisse restaurant in Berkeley, California, gained steam in the 1990s and 2000s. People not only wanted new tastes, they wanted – in fact, demanded – fresh, seasonal, local ingredients.

The experimentation and thought processes of the restaurant kitchen started to bleed over to the bar. A few forward-thinking bartenders in big cities such as London and New York

Customers sitting at the bar can choose from a massive selection of amari displayed on the back wall at Amor y Amargo, the first amaro and bitters bar in the United States.

began using ingredients like fresh-squeezed citrus, sought out classic liqueurs such as crème de mûre and started tinkering with old recipes. As for the Martini, sweet vodka versions still reigned, but traditional gin versions accented (not overpowered) by liqueurs also started to appear. Along with Dick Bradsell, bartender Salvatore Calabrese at the Library Bar in the Lanesborough Hotel led the charge in London for more elegant, restrained drinks. His Breakfast Martini featured gin, triple sec, orange marmalade and citrus. In New York at the Rainbow Room, Dale DeGroff – the most influential bartender on the American bar scene in the 1990s (and today still) – created the Ritz, a twist on the champagne cocktail that incorporated Cointreau and maraschino.

In time, the chef-forward mindset of elevating individual ingredients, as well as the quest to create new flavour combinations, slowly transferred to the bar; often chefs specifically sought out cocktails that complemented their menus' flavours. As drinks started to mirror the food and health trends of the time, sugar stepped down as the star player and became a supporting, but still essential, character in the interplay of ingredients. A shining example came from Emeryville, California, a small town around the corner from Berkeley's Chez Panisse. There, at the Townhouse Restaurant, bartender Paul Harrington sought out historic drinks and reimagined them for the modern, gourmet customer. His 1993 creation of the now-classic Jasmine took the Prohibition-era Pegu Club cocktail (gin, curaçao, lime, bitters) and transformed it with a whisper of bitter Campari, one of the few amari that were well known in the United States at the time.

Global Connectivity

As chefs and bartenders sought out new or reimagined ingredients and experiences, a broad, powerful catalyst was beginning to transform all facets of society: the World Wide Web. From bulletin boards, to user groups, to single-subject websites, the Internet of the 1990s created virtual communities where like minded people could gather to learn about and discuss everything from music, to collectibles, to cocktails. Among the most influential of the cocktail communities was DrinkBoy. Created by Microsoft employee Robert Hess in the late 1990s, the site promoted Hess's longstanding love of cocktails to a broad audience.

Soon after DrinkBoy debuted, Hess created a discussion forum that attracted bartenders from all corners of the globe. As Hess recalls,

> It is hard to imagine it these days, but back then bartenders and cocktail enthusiasts only had little more than people in their local physical vicinity to rely on for information ... A bartender who wanted to dig deeper than that was on their own and would often assume they were pretty much alone in their interests.

A core group, essentially a 'who's who' of the early cocktail renaissance, emerged, trading information and resources. Hess lists Gary 'Gaz' Regan, Dale DeGroff, Audrey Saunders, David Wondrich, Jared Brown, Anistatia Miller, Ted Haigh, Jeff Berry, Phillip Duff, Angus Winchester and Martin Doudoroff, among many others. Discussions often turned to liqueurs such as maraschino, which was next-to-impossible to obtain in the United States at the time. (Audrey Saunders, owner of the now-closed Pegu Club, went so far as to help find a distributor so she could acquire the liqueur for use at Pegu and, in turn, made it available to other bars in the United States.)

In a DrinkBoy post from 4 June 2000 entitled 'Extinct Liqueurs', cocktail historian Ted Haigh expressed his 'fascination' for what he called 'the dinosaurs of mixology'. Among these were Crème d'Yvette, Swedish Punsch and Forbidden Fruit, all of which are once again available. Hess's forum, as well as others including Paul Harrington's 'Cocktail Time' for *Wired*'s website and Ted Haigh's cocktailDB.com, were some of the earliest and most vital influencers in the arena.

As the Internet's offerings grew, and access became more common around the globe, websites offered valuable resources such as scans of old cocktail books and databases of recipes, while secure commercial transactions made international goods more accessible, and email allowed for immediate communication. Spirits and cocktail culture started to enjoy a network of like-minded souls. Thus, when the cocktail renaissance began, ideas, products and people created a real-time synergy, encouraging advances in technique, discussions about production

Disaronno Velvet is a cream-style version of the brand's popular almond liqueur. Launched in 2020, the liqueur advertisement still highlights the brand's Italian heritage with the slogan 'The New Dolcevita'.

and selections of historical materials. With its far-reaching influence and ability to connect people around the globe at the touch of a button, today's Internet has become a modern version of the Gutenberg press for the world spirits community.

Party Like It's 1999

In the years leading up to the new millennium, the wider bartending world, rather than a small contingent of enthusiasts, was starting to see the possibilities that well-crafted cocktails and fine ingredients could offer. Along with innovations in cuisine and the Internet, a combination of factors set the wheels in motion for the craft cocktail movement that would explode in the 2000s. In New York and London, pioneering bartenders such as Dale DeGroff and Dick Bradsell had become mentors to the next generation of mixologists, who looked at the profession as a career, not just a summer job. Historic and modern cocktail recipes started to show up more frequently in magazines, exposing the public to a fresh spectrum of flavours. More often than not, these flavours would include liqueurs. As the 2000s arrived, these liqueurs – both old and new styles – would become easier to come by.

While these changes happened gradually from the late 1990s into the early 2000s, there is arguably one specific date that changed the future of bartending culture in the United States. On New Year's Eve 1999, a nondescript, hole-in-the-wall bar with a no-reservations policy and a set of steadfast rules of conduct quietly opened its doors on New York's Lower East Side. The somewhat-prophetic name of the bar was Milk & Honey, which unintentionally launched the modern 'speakeasy'-style bar. Although owner and bartender Sasha Petraske disliked that label, his creation was at the forefront of the first generation of modern craft cocktail bars, starting in New York and progressing across the United States and around the world.

Establishments such as Milk & Honey begat a new era of bartenders who were voracious to recapture the lost alchemy of their craft. They, along with a growing cadre of enthusiasts, created demand for craft cocktail books, both historical and modern. Books such as Harrington's *Cocktail: The Drinks Bible for the 21st Century* (1998), William Grimes's cocktail history *Straight Up or on the Rocks* (2001), DeGroff's *The Craft of the Cocktail* (2002) and Ted Haigh's *Vintage Spirits and Forgotten Cocktails* (2004) brought the world of classic drinks, and the liqueurs that played essential roles in them, to a waiting public.

Then, in 2007, David Wondrich released *Imbibe!*, recounting the life of Jerry Thomas and highlighting the drinks in Thomas's *Bar-Tender's Guide*. In doing so, Wondrich created the Johnny Appleseed of cocktail culture. Thomas was a hero from the past who put a luminous name and face to the unfolding bibulous revolution. Bartenders zealously started shaking and stirring classic recipes. Distillers enthusiastically worked to re-introduce old spirits styles. Savvy business folk sought out brands that often had a single country of origin, and thus not easily available, bringing them to a larger market. Instead of supply leading to demand, demand inspired supply.

In the early to mid-2000s, several independent American companies – Haus Alpenz, Tempus Fugit and the Cooper Spirits Company – spoke to this demand. In another decade, they might not have succeeded. When Eric Seed established Haus Alpenz in 2005, the craft cocktail culture was still a somewhat underground movement, much of it centred on New York and London. In the United States, Seed recalls that flavoured vodkas and big brands ruled the roost, and 'sweet' was the dominant flavour, with liqueurs such as Tuaca, Midori and Rumple Minze (a peppermint schnapps) leading in popularity.

Tempus Fugit Spirits is dedicated to the glory of the well-made cocktail.

Our goal is to source and recreate rare spirits and liqueurs from the pages of history to satisfy the demands of the most discerning connoisseur. Our focus is on what is often called a cocktail 'modifier'; those spirit-based ingredients used to transform whisky, gin, rum, etc. into a cocktail. The quality of the products that we represent clearly expresses why these award-winning brands stand at the very pinnacle of their categories.

Tempus Fugit Spirits advertisement, including the liqueur product line.

Eschewing mass-market appeal, Seed focused on rarefied European liqueurs and, later, spirits. One of his earliest imports was the pinecone-based Zirbenz Stone pine liqueur, produced in the Austrian Alps. 'At their best, liqueurs are made to optimize both the flavours they are representing and their intended use,' says Seed of why liqueurs were and still are so important to the bar world. 'They are a great medium for delivering both sweet and sometimes difficult to extract flavours, whether herbal or bitter notes. What's essential is that they are consistent.'

Seed's contribution to modern liqueur culture in America is undeniable. Among the products he is responsible for bringing to the United States are Salers gentian aperitif and the family of Rothman & Winter liqueurs. Most recently, in 2012, Seed worked with master blender Henrik Facile to engineer a modern version of Swedish Punsch, having discovered that punsch was employed 'in some of the most famous, historic drinks' such as the Boomerang (rye, Swedish Punsch, dry vermouth, lemon juice) and the Diki-Diki (Calvados, Swedish Punsch, grapefruit juice). Seed's version emulates original nineteenth-century recipes, which use the Indonesian sugarcane spirit Batavia arrack (also one of his imports), as well as a small portion of fermented red rice. A surprising addition to Seed's portfolio is hay liqueurs, traditional in northern Italy, Austria and some parts of Bavaria.

Around the same time as Haus Alpenz arrived, Tempus Fugit Spirits came on the scene, making its name as an importer of several French and Swiss absinthes, once the U.S. import ban was lifted. In the following years, founders John Troia and Peter Schaf expanded their focus to include pre-Prohibition liqueurs. Using what they call 'nineteenth-century protocols' – no artificial flavours or colours, no industrial production – they became one of the earliest, modern American producers of old-world, artisan liqueurs. Their line now includes crème de cacao, menthe, noyau, banane and violette, as well as an amaro called Fernet Del Frate.

While Haus Alpenz and Tempus Fugit were building up steam by satisfying the niche for recherché and historical styles, Robert Cooper, a scion of the Jacquin liqueur company family, founded his eponymous Cooper Spirits Company in 2006. Eager to make a personal mark on the burgeoning modern liqueur business, he created St-Germain, an elderflower liqueur that rocketed to stardom almost as soon as it was released. The slightly floral, softly sweet cordial had everything one could want in a liqueur. The novel flavour profile, evocative Belle Époque bottle design and savvy, sexy marketing machine created a seismic shift in the spirits world.

After its release, St-Germain became the darling of mixologists and played a starring role in a myriad of cocktails. It was on so many menus in so many forms that it became known in the industry as 'the bartender's ketchup'. At a certain point, the 'ketchup' label became, perhaps unfairly, a bit pejorative, but St-Germain remains a fixture on bar shelves and a watershed in the liqueur business. Robert Simonson summed up this influence in a *New York Times* article on 29 December 2009. In it, he

Hpnotiq became a fixture of the club scene of the 2000s and was mentioned frequently in music of the time.

unequivocally stated that 'the elderflower-based elixir with the sui generis floral flavor almost single-handedly invigorated the moribund liqueur category.'

For every craft spirit and liqueur that appeared, there were brands that appealed to a more mass-market, party-orientated drinker who did not always want liqueur in a cocktail, but rather to drink on its own. In 2001 French vodka- and cognac-based Hpnotiq caught the public eye in part due to its unmistakable neon turquoise colour and juicy tropical fruit flavour. It soon became the darling of rappers such as Kanye West and Sean Combs, many of whom touted the erotic qualities of the drink that they often sipped with 'Henny', their nickname for Hennessy cognac. The liqueur also became popular in a green-hued cocktail fittingly called the Incredible Hulk that combined Hpnotiq with cognac, lime and bitters.

Meanwhile, despite its roots as a traditional German digestif, Jägermeister continued to be a de rigueur party shot. That position was challenged in 2007 by a cinnamon-flavoured schnapps called Fireball. Originally known by the ungainly name of Dr. McGillicuddy's Fireball Whisky, the liqueur received a rebrand when Canadian whiskey producer Seagram's sold the product to the Sazerac Company. As part of its inspired marketing strategy, Sazerac shortened the name, slapped a fire-breathing devil on the label and invented the tag line 'Tastes Like Heaven, Burns Like Hell'. Much like St-Germain, Fireball illustrates how a well-calibrated marketing machine can buoy a brand's success. Fireball demonstrated the potential power of the 'brand ambassador', an individual who is part educator and part sales representative. Fireball's ambassador Richard Pomes, who targeted towns with energetic bar cultures and sold Fireball as a party shot, is often credited with the brand's seemingly overnight success.

Equally eager to cash in on the continued market share of populist liqueurs that promoted a fun party vibe, many vodka brands stepped into the spotlight with sweetened vodkas. Some flavoured vodkas are specifically classified as 'infused', meaning that they contain infusions of natural essences such as citrus or cucumber and are without added sugar. In stark contrast, sweetly concentrated, dessert-style vodkas, which started to arrive on the market around 2010, can use natural or artificial flavours, as well as sweetener. From familiar flavours such as chocolate or caramel to more kitschy ones such as birthday cake and marshmallow, these vodkas are, for all intents, liqueurs.

Boom Time

Much of liqueur's current fortunes must be seen through the lens of the American cocktail and the international culture it has birthed. While liqueurs have long been enjoyed on their own in many countries, they take on a new dimension as modifiers or even as judiciously used star players in cocktails. In many ways, it is because of cocktails and their concomitant flavour demands that the twenty-first-century liqueur world has grown so exponentially.

The rediscovery of the cocktails that Jerry Thomas and his bartending compatriots chronicled in their recipe books awakened the need for a vast array of historical, often-difficult-to-acquire liqueurs. This demand is now satisfied on a once-unimaginable level. Today numerous craft expressions of generic styles, such as crème de menthe and curaçao, offer an alternative to mass-produced versions, which are often made with artificial, low-quality ingredients. Likewise, liqueurs that were frequently called for in turn-of-the-century bartending books no longer languish in obscurity, thanks to numerous independent producers. In 2016 drinks industry veteran Giuseppe Gallo created Italicus di Bergamotto, a centuries-old style of rosolio. Currently,

OM Chocolate Liqueur, made in the United States from sugarcane spirit, macerated with fair trade, organic chocolate. The company, OM, has also created a tinned cocktail that blends their product with cold brew coffee in an easily sippable riff on the Espresso Martini.

Foss Distillery's Björk Birch Liqueur from Iceland is made with indigenous birch (the Icelandic word for 'birch' is *björk*).

Heirloom Spirits produces the only American-made alchermes, while Lee Spirits recently researched historical documents and tasted old bottles of Forbidden Fruit to create the first modern version on the market.

Currently, heritage brands and styles are experiencing a huge boost in popularity and demand, allowing them to expand their

Nixta corn liqueur, one of many unexpected flavours showing up in new liqueurs.

lines and distribution. Products from historic French liqueur houses such as Marie Brizard, Giffard and Mathilde have become easier to find, particularly in the United States. Trailblazers such as Bols and DeKuyper have continued to expand their offerings. Italy's vast array of amari, as well as a myriad of other indigenous styles, have attained global distribution thanks to both large and small spirits companies, as well as multiple spirits sellers online. Even countries not generally thought of as large-scale, commercial liqueur producers have slowly begun to contribute products. For example, the spice-centric Licor Armada, from the Indian state of Goa, is the first of that country's liqueurs to be lauded internationally. Other liqueurs from India are also reaching the world stage, including the Rajasthan region's royal heritage liqueurs whose recipes date back hundreds of years.

As the cocktail renaissance has settled into itself, craft bartenders have started to let their metaphorical hair down, re-imagining and even embracing retro cocktails, which, in turn, have contributed to the visibility and popularity of the required liqueurs. The Harvey Wallbanger's Galliano, the Grasshopper's and Stinger's crème de menthe and the Amaretto Sour's eponymous almond liqueur are but a few examples. And with every traditional style comes an out-there wild child such as Ancho Reyes chilli liqueur and Tamworth Distilling's Black Trumpet Blueberry Cordial.

Likewise, where certain categories were once ruled by one brand, they now offer a slew of choices. While Cointreau and Grand Marnier are often the go-to orange liqueurs, multiple other brands such as Luxardo's Triplum and Pierre Ferrand Dry Curaçao have emerged. Similarly, coffee category king Kahlúa now has upstart siblings in Mr Black from Australia, Galliano Ristretto and Jägermeister Cold Brew. And almost every English gin brand from the old-school Plymouth to the modern Sipsmith has jumped on the sloe gin train.

As dull as statistics can be, they don't lie; indeed, they offer a magnifying glass on liqueur's current profitability and overall influence in the drinks world. From an American perspective, DISCUS, the Distilled Spirits Council of the United States, offers a comparison. In 2015 cordial imports amounted to $864 million; in 2019 that number had risen to just over $1 billion. Craft cocktails appear on menus around the world, even in chain restaurants. And bartenders, once beholden to the rigid specifications of classic cocktails, have embarked on a new era of experimentation, creating modern classics and riffing on old ones. The only requirement now is that flavours be delicious and satisfy our innate desire for pleasure. Our ape ancestors would be proud.

Australia's Mr Black Mezcal Cask Coffee Liqueur in collaboration with Ilegal Mezcal, launched in 2022, joins its original basic coffee liqueur release from 2013.

The Chartreuse Swizzle, a modern classic. When bartender Marcovaldo Dionysos created this drink in 2003, he put the spotlight on the Chartreuse and demonstrated how the right liqueur could easily be the star of the show.

Liqueur's most alluring trait is grounded in its ability to transcend categorization. Beyond the use of sugar and flavourings, liqueurs can employ any spirit, from rum to brandy, gin to tequila, as their base. They can be delicately sweet or shockingly bitter. Their botanical constituents can range from fruits to nuts, roots to bark and everything in between.

Even more fascinating is the breadth of this sweetened spirit's evolution. Its history reaches further back in time, touches on more cultures and exists during more major historical moments than any other individual spirit. The beginnings of liqueur date back to 8000 BCE, when sugar, liqueur's defining ingredient, was likely first domesticated in New Guinea. Distillation, necessary for all spirits production, most probably dates to 2000 BCE in China or Egypt. The Spice Routes, which transported sugar and spices from East Asia to the European West, flourished as early as 1500 BCE, eventually involving peoples as diverse as the Ethiopians, the Turks, the Dutch and the Italians. Each step of liqueur's growth has been influenced by specific geography, inventions and people. And, with each sip, we can taste that history.

The first liqueurs, known as cordials, took their name from the medieval Latin term *cordialis*, meaning 'of the heart' and were specifically considered medicinal elixirs. But, as society became less about survival and more about enjoyment, these elixirs evolved and took on a more recreational role. They became less of a necessity and more of an indulgence. It is far from coincidental that *cordialis* evolved into the adjective 'cordial', which connotes warmth, comfort and friendliness.

With their ancient roots, cordials and liqueurs are the standard-bearers of what spirits have offered us throughout the ages: conviviality and celebration. Indeed, whether medicinal or recreational, liqueurs have played a crucial social role for longer than any other spirit category. They offer a bridge throughout the ages, linking the Golden Age of Islam to the Age of Exploration, Catherine de' Medici to Charles Dickens, saloons to speakeasies. With their variety of flavours, textures and alcohol bases, they are the most diverse – and the most useful – of all spirits categories. Enjoyed on their own or used judiciously as modifiers, they transform any drink they touch in ways that spirits like gin or whisky cannot. Indeed, without liqueur, an entire world of punches, shooters and cocktails – both classic and modern – would not exist: just a little something to think about while you sip your Last Word, Singapore Sling or Espresso Martini.

Recipes

Historic Recipes:
Pre-Prohibition to the 1970s

Alexander (1916), Brandy Alexander (1937)

The original Alexander used gin and shows up in Hugo Ensslin's *Recipes for Mixed Drinks* (1916). Over the years, brandy became the favoured spirit, but numerous variations abound, often substituting other liqueurs for the crème de cacao. The equal-parts recipe can be tinkered with depending on your preference for more or less spirit, liqueur or cream.

> 30 ml (1 fl. oz) gin (original) or 30 ml (1 fl. oz) cognac-style brandy
> 30 ml (1 fl. oz) crème de cacao
> 30 ml (1 fl. oz) sweet cream

Shake all ingredients with ice until cold and frothy. Strain into a cocktail glass. Dust with fresh grated nutmeg.

Amaretto Sour (1970s)
Courtesy of Jeffrey Morgenthaler

The Amaretto Sour achieved popularity in the 1970s, with its rather unremarkable combination of amaretto liqueur and citrus, which, at that time, was likely in the form of bottled sour mix. The problem with this drink is that the liqueur-centric character can make for an extremely cloying cocktail.

In the early 2000s, Portland, Oregon, bartender and author of *Drinking Distilled* Jeffrey Morgenthaler spent a good deal of time mulling over the state of the Amaretto Sour. Of his version, which is considered by many to be the definitive one today, he says, 'It was more of a reaction to this idea [that] some drinks are inherently good, and some drinks are inherently bad.' Morganthaler's problem with the original Amaretto Sour was that the liqueur plays the key role, but its low ABV makes it impossible to create a balanced drink. This recipe is Morganthaler's solution.

> 45 ml (1½ fl. oz) amaretto
> 22 ml (¾ fl. oz) cask-proof bourbon
> 30 ml (1 fl. oz) lemon juice
> 1 tsp 2:1 simple syrup (sugar:water)
> 15 ml (½ fl. oz) egg white, lightly beaten

Combine ingredients in a cocktail shaker and shake without ice or (even better) use an immersion blender to combine and froth. Shake well with cracked ice. Strain over fresh ice into an old-fashioned glass. Garnish with lemon peel and brandied cherries, if desired. As Morgenthaler states, 'Serve and grin like an idiot as your friends freak out.' They will.

Bijou, Ritz Version (1936)

The original recipe for the Bijou calls for green Chartreuse and sweet vermouth. This version, which arrived in 1936 at the Ritz Hotel in Paris, is surprising on several levels. Without the orange liqueur, this is, for all intents, a Martini. The addition of the orange liqueur softens the stoutness of the spirit-forward original and spotlights just how powerfully a liqueur can transform a drink.

60 ml (2 fl. oz) dry gin
15 ml (½ fl. oz) orange liqueur (Cointreau suggested)
15 ml (½ fl. oz) dry vermouth
dash orange bitters

Combine all ingredients in a mixing glass. Fill the glass with ice and stir vigorously for about 30 seconds until well chilled. Strain into a coupe glass and garnish with a high-quality maraschino cherry.

Boomerang (1930s)

With minimal ingredients, the Boomerang is an elegant recipe, and it demonstrates why Swedish Punsch is such a luscious liqueur. While bourbon or Canadian whiskey are sometimes substituted for rye, the recipe is essentially the same, appearing in *The Savoy Cocktail Book* (1930), *The Café Royal Cocktail Book* (1937) and Trader Vic's 1947 *Bartender's Guide*, among others. Throughout the decades, the Boomerang cocktail has morphed into a wide assortment of recipes that are a far cry from the original.

30 ml (1 fl. oz) rye whiskey
30 ml (1 fl. oz) Swedish Punsch
30 ml (1 fl. oz) dry vermouth
dash lemon juice
dash Angostura bitters

Place all ingredients in an ice-filled shaker and shake vigorously for about 30 seconds. Strain into a cocktail glass.

El Diablo (1946)

One of the few tequila drinks from the first half of the twentieth century, El Diablo was originally named 'the Mexican Diablo' in Trader Vic's *Bartender's Guide*. The lime and ginger beer offer a refreshing zing, while the cassis adds an unexpected pop of flavour.

45 ml (1½ fl. oz) reposado tequila
15 ml (½ fl. oz) crème de cassis
22 ml (¾ fl. oz) fresh squeezed lime juice
60 ml (2 fl. oz) ginger beer

Shake the first three ingredients with ice until well chilled, approximately 30 seconds. Strain into a Collins (or highball) glass. Add ice. Top with ginger beer. Garnish with a lime slice if desired.

Fedora (1888)

Dating back to Harry Johnson's 1888 edition of his *Bartender's Manual*, the Fedora is a mostly forgotten cocktail that deserves a comeback. Named for the fedora hat that actress Sarah Bernhardt wore in the 1882 play of the same name, the original drink recipe called for a full ounce (30 ml) of orange liqueur. Where liqueurs generally function as an accent, here the orange liqueur shines through, marrying all the ingredients together. Variations change the proportions, particularly of the orange liqueur.

1 tbsp icing (powdered) sugar
1 tsp water
30 ml (1 fl. oz) cognac-style brandy
15 ml (½ fl. oz) amber rum
15 ml (½ fl. oz) rye whiskey
30 ml (1 fl. oz) orange liqueur, like Cointreau

In a mixing glass, combine the powdered sugar and the water. Add the remaining ingredients, fill the mixing glass with ice and shake until well chilled, approximately 30 seconds. Strain into a rocks glass filled with crushed ice or a single, large ice cube, if preferred. Garnish with a lemon wheel and add a straw if served with crushed ice.

Hanky-Panky (early 1900s)

Created by Ada Coleman, the Savoy Hotel American Bar's first female bartender, this is essentially a tweak on the famous Martinez cocktail, which was the precursor to the Martini. The former drink employed maraschino and bitters. Coleman's use of Fernet-Branca not only turns the Martinez profile on its ear, but illustrates how even the smallest addition of the right liqueur can alter a drink's profile immeasurably.

45 ml (1½ fl. oz) dry gin
2 dashes Fernet-Branca
45 ml (1½ fl. oz) sweet vermouth

Pour all ingredients into a mixing glass filled with ice. Stir vigorously for about 30 seconds. Strain into a cocktail glass.

Rusty Nail (1937 or later)

History is murky on the origin of this cocktail; it could date from as early as 1937 or as late as the 1960s, when it was incredibly popular. The simplicity of this drink – Scotch whisky and Drambuie – might make one think it is unremarkable. But in those simple two ingredients lies the Rusty Nail's allure. The whiskey base of the Drambuie, Gaelic for 'the drink that satisfies', seamlessly melds with the Scotch, while the honey and herbal notes soften the whisky's profile. Adding a large cube of ice allows the drink to dilute slowly, softening it as it is consumed. Use unpeated Scotch, so the smokiness doesn't overpower the liqueur.

45 ml (1½ fl. oz) Scotch whisky
22 ml (¾ fl. oz) Drambuie

Add the two ingredients to a mixing glass and fill with ice. Stir until well chilled, and then strain into a rocks glass with one large ice cube.

The Widow's Kiss (1895)

First recorded in George Kappeler's *Modern American Drinks*, this is a true pre-Prohibition gem that showcases two potent herbal liqueurs in all their glory. A strong and viscous cocktail, the Widow's Kiss encourages slow, contemplative sipping, preferably in front of a cosy fire.

45 ml (1½ fl. oz) calvados
22 ml (¾ fl. oz) Chartreuse
22 ml (¾ fl. oz) Bénédictine
2 dashes Angostura bitters

Add all ingredients to a cocktail shaker filled with ice and shake until well chilled, about 30 seconds. Strain into a coupe-style glass. Garnish with a high-quality maraschino cherry.

Modern Drinks

Bramble (1980s)

One of Dick Bradsell's best-known cocktail recipes, this drink now appears on menus around the world. It has become a modern classic.

60 ml (2 fl. oz) gin
30 ml (1 fl. oz) lemon juice, freshly squeezed
2 tsp simple syrup
15 ml (½ fl. oz) crème de mûre

Add the gin, lemon juice and simple syrup to a shaker filled with ice and shake until well chilled, about 30 seconds. Fill a Collins or old-fashioned glass with crushed ice, creating a dome of ice on top. Drizzle the crème de mûre over the crushed ice. Garnish with blackberries and a sprig of mint or lemon slice.

Chartreuse Swizzle (2003)
Courtesy of Marcovaldo Dionysos (bartender and cocktail geek)

As Marco recalls, he came up with this drink for the Fifth Annual Chartreuse Competition in San Francisco. 'I wanted to try something new, so I went [in] a tropical direction. Falernum was still mostly unknown and was my "secret weapon" in a few other contests. I won the competition, but it took several years to catch on as falernum became more widely available.' This tiki twist on the traditional swizzle, with its surprising herbal hit from the Chartreuse, is now a modern classic.

7 ml (¼ fl. oz) green Chartreuse
15 ml (½ fl. oz) Velvet Falernum
30 ml (1 fl. oz) pineapple juice
22 ml (¾ fl. oz) lime juice

Place all ingredients in a shaker filled with ice and shake until well chilled, about 30 seconds. Strain into an ice-filled Collins glass. Garnish with a pineapple spear and a lime wheel.

Espresso Martini (original version, 1980s)

Another Dick Bradsell modern classic that shows just how influential Bradsell was in London and on global cocktail culture at large.

60 ml (2 fl. oz) vodka
15 ml (½ fl. oz) coffee liqueur

7.5 ml (¼ fl. oz) 1:1 simple syrup
30 ml (1 fl. oz) ristretto shot (short pull) of espresso

Place all ingredients in an ice-filled cocktail shaker, espresso last. Shake until well chilled, about 30 seconds. Strain into a V-shaped Martini glass (to capture the 1980s retro vibe) and garnish with three coffee beans. Enjoy the caffeine kick.

Her Word (2000s)
Courtesy of Haus Alpenz

This tequila sour gets its fresh sweetness from the peach liqueur and a hint of bitterness from the Cocchi Americano.

22 ml (¾ fl. oz) blanco tequila
22 ml (¾ fl. oz) Cocchi Americano Blanco
22 ml (¾ fl. oz) peach liqueur, such as Rothman & Winter
22 ml (¾ fl. oz) lemon juice, strained

Add all ingredients to an ice-filled shaker and shake until well chilled, about 30 seconds. Strain into a cocktail glass. Garnish with lemon peel.

Silk Sheets (2016)
Courtesy of Heirloom Liqueurs

As the first company to produce an alchermes in the United States, Heirloom has made a notable contribution to bringing back a forgotten spirit. Of the cocktail, the crew at Heirloom explains, 'This cocktail gets its name from the ancient method of using dyed silk to color the first iterations of Alchermes. Mezcal connects to the origins of cochineal in Mexico. Cognac references the popularity of Alchermes in France, introduced to them by the Medicis . . . The cocktail is at once a harmony of earthy, smoky, bright, fruity, floral and aromatic. The magic of Alchermes is that it can stand up against bold ingredients and bind seemingly disparate flavours/ aromatics together.'

22 ml (¾ fl. oz) fresh squeezed lemon juice
15 ml (½ fl. oz) simple syrup
22 ml (¾ fl. oz) mezcal espadín jóven
22 ml (¾ fl. oz) vs cognac
15 ml (½ fl. oz) Heirloom Alchermes
1 dash orange bitters (preferably Bittercube)

Add all the ingredients to a cocktail shaker and fill with ice. Shake with a fluid, strong motion and strain into cocktail glass. Express an orange peel over the glass and discard peel. Serve with French burnt peanuts, a nod to France and Alchermes's confectionary past.

Too Soon? (2011)
Courtesy of Sam Ross, Attaboy

Ross created this less-is-more cocktail in 2011 while working at Sasha Petraske's groundbreaking Milk & Honey in New York. Taking a cue from the standard gin sour, Ross added Cynar and some orange slices to create a cocktail that contains just a wisp of the rather aggressive artichoke amaro. As to the cocktail's genesis, Ross says, 'I created the drink when we had some excessive cases of Cynar in the basement due to an ordering snafu. While Sasha loved the Cynar logo, he very much disliked the product (and all things bitter in general). When I made this drink for him, he begrudgingly acknowledged its deliciousness and we were slowly able to move through that backlog of Cynar!'

30 ml (1 fl. oz) gin
30 ml (1 fl. oz) Cynar
22 ml (¾ fl. oz) fresh lemon juice
15 ml (½ fl. oz) simple syrup (1:1)
2 orange slices

Add all ingredients to a cocktail shaker and shake vigorously until well chilled. Strain into a chilled coupe glass without garnish.

Vetiver Vieux Carré (2023)
Courtesy of Alex Kratena, bartender at Tayēr + Elementary.
Created for *Liqueur: A Global History*

The traditional Vieux Carré uses Bénédictine as the defining liqueur. Kratena's Muyu liqueur, from his line of liqueurs, adds 'earthy, woody, tobacco-like aromatics'.

25 ml (¾ fl. oz) cognac VSOP
25 ml (¾ fl. oz) sweet vermouth
1½ tsp Muyu Vetiver Gris
dash Peychaud's bitters

Combine all ingredients in a mixing glass, add ice and stir until cold and diluted. Serve over ice in a rocks glass.

Waterproof Watch (*c.* 2015)
Courtesy of Sother Teague, Amor y Amargo, New York

This is a 'light-bodied and refreshing' Negroni variation that demonstrates how amari can complement and elevate each other. Aperol is a softer, bitter orange amaro than the usual Campari, while amaro Montenegro is one of the gentler amari.

45 ml (1½ fl. oz) London dry gin
22 ml (¾ fl. oz) amaro Montenegro
22 ml (¾ fl. oz) Aperol
2 dashes DeGroff Pimento Bitters

Stir all ingredients in an ice-filled mixing glass. Strain into a rocks glass with a large ice cube and orange twist.

White Negroni (2001)

Originally created in 2001 by London bartender Wayne Collins at the VinExpo trade show in Bordeaux, France. By focusing on French ingredients, Collins reinvented the traditional, Campari-forward Negroni. Because Suze and Lillet were hard to come by, the cocktail took some time to catch on. One of the first places the cocktail appeared was on the menu at Audrey Saunders's Pegu Club in the USA, where Saunders evangelized the wonders of gin at a time when no one wanted it. The modern recipe is more gin-forward and less Suze.

45 ml (1½ fl. oz) dry gin
30 ml (1 fl. oz) Lillet Blanc
30 ml (1 fl. oz) Suze gentian liqueur

Add all ingredients to an ice-filled mixing glass and stir until well chilled, about 15 to 20 seconds. Strain into a rocks glass filled with ice. Garnish with a lemon twist.

Woodland Flor (2023)
Courtesy of Sebastian Hamilton-Mudge.
Created for *Liqueur: A Global History*

With the nutty, dry amontillado sherry substituting for dry vermouth, this drink has the feel of a Martini, but is more easy-drinking. As Hamilton-Mudge explains, 'Adding the flavour of stone fruit to the light, crisp notes of gin and the woodland floor notes of sherry creates a drink in perfect balance.'

60 ml (2 fl. oz) dry gin
15 ml (½ fl. oz) amontillado sherry
1 tsp of apricot liqueur, such as Mathilde or Giffard

Stir all ingredients in an ice-filled mixing glass until well chilled, about 30 seconds. Strain into a cocktail glass.

Appendix:
Catalogue of World Liqueurs

Many liqueurs have been covered in this book; it would be an insurmountable task to cover every liqueur that exists. New products are released every year, while multiple countries and regions produce generic styles that often do not became widely accessible outside the country in question. As such, the list below includes a selection of products from around the globe – noting their point of origin and their style or primary flavour. If they are proprietary (that is, brand name) products, this will be delineated as (P) after the name. There are many small, artisan brands that are not mentioned here that are worth seeking out by region, country and state. Apologies are due for not being able to include everyone.

A Selection of Producers of Multiple Liqueurs

The Bitter Truth (USA)
Bols (Netherlands)
Boudier (France)
Briottet (France)
De Kuyper (Netherlands, USA)
Drillaud (France)
Giffard (France)
Hiram Walker (USA)
Joseph Cartron (France)
Luxardo (Italy)
Marie Brizard (France)

Mathilde (France)
Rothman & Winter (Austria)
Tamworth Distilling/Art in the Age (USA)
Tempus Fugit (USA)
Vedrenne (France)

Examples of Crème Liqueur Styles

de banane (banana)
de cacao (chocolate, vanilla)
de cassis/de cassis de Bourgogne (blackcurrant)
de cerise (cherry)
de fraise (strawberry)
de framboise (raspberry)
de menthe (mint)
de mûre (blackberry)
de noyau (almond/cherry/peach stones)
de pêche (peach)
de violette (violet flowers)

Liqueurs of Bark, Flowers, Leaves, Plants

alloro bay laurel leaves (Puglia, Italy)
Araceli Marigold (P) marigold flowers (USA)
Armand Guy 'Le Vert Sapin' (P) fir tree buds (Pontalier, France)
cantueso alicantino *Thymus moroderi* (local name: cantueso)
    (Alicante, Spain)
Chareau (P) eau de vie base with aloe (primary botanical),
    cucumber, lemon peel, muskmelon, spearmint (USA)
Chios mastiha masticha chiou (resinous sap from Schinias tree
    (Chios, Greece)
Crème D' Yvette (P) Parma violets, rose petals, various berries
    (France)
Fjallagrasa Moss Schnapps (P) indigenous moss (Iceand)
Foss Björk (P) birch bark with birch syrup (Iceland)

Goldschläger (p) cinnamon with thin gold leaf flakes (Switzerland)

Green Bar Distillery Poppy Amaro (p) poppies plus dandelion, gentian artichoke and others (USA)

Kaapse Honeybush (p) honeybush (similar to rooibos) (South Africa)

Latsche young pinecones (Southern Tyrol, Italy)

Parfait Amour usually a curaçao base with violets, roses, citrus and vanilla (originally France, now multiple producers)

rozulin indigenous roses (*Rosa* × *centifolia*) (Dubrovnik, Croatia)

St-Germain (p) elderflowers (France)

Coffee Liqueurs

12th Hawaii Distiller's Kona Coffee (p) distilled honey base, Kona coffee beans (Kailua-Kona, Hawaii)

Borghetti (p) robusta or arabica coffee beans (Ancona, Italy)

café licor/café de Alcoy Arabica coffee beans (Alcoy, Spain)

Kahlúa (p) rum base with arabica coffee beans and vanilla beans (Mexico)

Mr Black Cold Brew (p) Arabica coffee beans (also produces coffee amaro, rum barrel and mezcal finishes) (Australia)

Sheridan's (p) two separate parts: coffee and chocolate with whiskey base, and vanilla cream liqueur (Dublin, Ireland)

St George Nola Coffee (p) Ethiopian Yirgacheffe coffee beans, chicory root and vanilla (USA)

Tia Maria (p) Jamaican rum base with coffee beans and vanilla (originally made in Jamaica, now made in Italy)

Chocolate Liqueurs

Ashanti Gold (p) produced by Peter Heering (Denmark)

Bicerin (p) chocolate with hazelnuts (Turin, Italy)

Bottega Gianduia Chocolate Cream (p) grappa base with chocolate and hazelnut paste (Italy)

crème de cacao whiskey or vodka base with cacao beans and
vanilla (originally France, now multiple distillers)

Dorda Double Chocolate (P) Chopin rye vodka with
milk and dark chocolate (Poland)

Godiva Dark Chocolate (P) dark chcoloate with candied
orange peel, black cherry and coffee (Belgium)

OM (P) chocolate and sea salt (USA)

Patrón XO Café Dark Cocoa (P) tequila base with chocolate
and coffee (Mexico)

Patron XO Cafe INCENDIO Chile Chocolate Liqueur (P)
tequila base with chocolate and chile (Mexico)

Sabra Chocolate Orange (P) dark chocolate and Jaffa oranges
(Israel)

Cream Liqueurs

Amarula (P) distilled marula (elephant tree) fruit with
cream (also raspberry, chocolate, African baobab,
Ethiopian coffee and vanilla spice flavours) (South Africa)

Baileys (P) Irish whiskey with Irish dairy cream with
chocolate and vanilla (also Espresso Cream, Red Velvet,
Strawberries & Cream, Almande, Salted Caramel) (Ireland)

Carolans (P) Irish whiskey with cream and honey (Ireland)

Columba Cream (P) single malt whiskey base with fresh
cream and honey (Scotland)

Disaronno Velvet (P) amaretto base with cream (Italy)

Dooley's (P) vodka with Dutch cream and Belgian toffee
(Germany)

Ezra Brooks (P) bourbon with cream (USA)

Guappa (P) brandy with DOP buffalo milk cream (Italy)

Magnum (P) Speyside single malt whiskey with cream
(Scotland)

RumChata (P) Caribbean rum base with spices and Wisconsin
dairy cream (USA)

Saint Brendan's (P) aged Irish whiskey with cream (Derry,
Northern Ireland)

Sangster's (P) aged rum with spices, fruit and cream (Jamaica)

Somrus Chai (P) rum base with cardamom, rose, saffron, pistachio, almond and turmeric with cream (also coffee and mango cream) (USA)

Sugarlands Distilling Appalachian Sippin' Cream (P) grain base with flavours that include dark chocolate coffee and butter pecan (USA)

Egg Liqueurs

advocaat eggs with brandy (Netherlands)

Ponche Crema (P) Venezulan eggnog (Venezuela)

rompope rum or brandy base with egg yolks and spices (Latin American eggnog) (Puebla de Zaragoza, Mexico)

vov (P) Marsala wine base with egg yolks and sugar (Padua, Italy)

Zabov (P) egg yolks (Ferrara, Italy)

Fruit Liqueurs

bargnolino   (known locally as bargnö or bargnòl) neutral spirit with sloe berries (Parma, Piacenza, Italy)

Bombay Bramble (P) gin base with blackberries and raspberries (England)

Chambord (P) Cognac base with black raspberries (France)

cherry bounce cherries (USA)

Cherry Heering brandy base with cherries and spices (Denmark)

DeKuyper Peachtree Schnapps (P) peaches (USA)

fragolino strawberry (Veneto, Italy)

ginjinha sour cheries (Portugal)

grappa di mirtilli (also called schwarzbeerschnaps) grappa spirit with blueberries (Trentino, South Tyrol, Italy)

Greenhook Beach Plum (P) gin base with New York Beach plums (USA)

Guignolet cherries (France)

Lakka (P) cloudberries (Finland)

Luxardo Sangue Morlacco (P) cherries (Padua, Italy)

maesil-ju soju (usually distilled from rice) with Asian plums (South Korea)

maraschino sour Marasca cherries (mostly Italy); proprietary brands include Luxardo, Lazzaroni, Boudier and Leopold Bros. (USA)

mirinello cherries (Torremaggiore, Puglia, Italy)

mirto red myrtle berries (Sardinia)

pacharán sloe berries in anise spirit (Navarre, Spain)

Pataka Açaí (P) açaí berries (Pataka also makes coffee, ginger, goji, pomegranate and quinoa liqueurs) (France)

Priqly (P) prickly pear (Malta)

RinQuinQuin (P) peach and peach leaves with white wine (Provence, France)

rượu sim rose myrtle berries (Phú Quốc, Vietnam)

sloe gin sloe berries (England); proprietary brands include Hayman's, Plymouth, Sipsmith

Ti-Toki (P) ti-toki berries (Auckland, New Zealand)

umeshu usually shōchū as base spirit with ume plums (Japan)

vișinată sour cherries (Romania)

xuxu (P) strawberries (Germany)

Zedda Piras (P) myrtle berries (Caligari, Italy)

Citrus Liqueurs

Agavero (P) tequila base with orange and agave nectar (Mexico)

Aurum (P) brandy base with orange infusion (Pescara, Italy)

curaçao orange (various types now used, originally Lahara orange); proprietary brands include Grand Marnier (France), Senior & Co. (Curaçao), Pierre Ferrand Dry Curaçao (France)

Drillaud (P) brandy base with orange (France)

fatourada tsipouro (pomace) base spirit with orange and spice (Kythira, Greece)

Grand Gala (P) Italian VSOP brandy with orange infusion (originally from Italy)

Hesperidina (P) orange (Buenos Aires, Argentina)

Italicus Rosolio de Bergamotto (P) bergamot with chamomile, lavender, gentian, yellow roses, melissa balm in Italian neutral spirit (England; rosolio is originally from Italy)

kitro citron leaves and neutral alcohol (Naxos, Greece)

limoncello traditionally sfusato lemon (southern Italy)

Mandarine Napoléon (P) tangerine (France)

Naranja (P) oranges (Mexico)

nespolino loquat seeds often with vanilla and cinnamon (Italy)

Patrón Citrónge (P) neutral grain spirit base with Jamaican and Haitian oranges (Mexico)

Rhum Clément Créole Shrubb (P) rhum agricole base with orange peels and spices (Martinique)

Solerno (P) blood orange (Italy)

Sukkah Hill Spirits Etrog (P) heirloom citrus (California, USA)

triple sec various types of oranges and alcohol bases; proprietary brand examples include Cointreau (France), Combier (France), Drillard (France), Lazzaroni Triplo (Italy), Luxardo Triplum (Italy)

Van der Hum (P) brandy or wine distillate with tangerine and spices (South Africa)

Vana Tallinn (P) rum-based with citrus, cinnamon and vanilla (Tallinn, Estonia)

Miscellaneous Fruit Liqueurs

DeKuyper Apple Pucker (P) apples (USA)

Destilería Bodega y Abasolo Nixta (P) corn (Mexico)

Kaapse Pittekou (P) granadilla (variant of passion fruit) pulp (South Africa)

Kalani (P) rum with coconut (Mérida, Mexico)

Lee Spirits Forbidden Fruit (P) grapefruit, honey, spices (USA)

Lichido (P) cognac base with lychee, white pear, guava (Cognac, France)

Licor Armada Asian spices and Portuguese fruit (Goa, India)
Malibu Rum (P) rum with coconut extract (Barbados)
Midori melon (Japan)
murtado guava (Chile)
nanassino prickly pear (Amalfi Coast, Cilento, Salento)
Pama (P) pomegranate juice (USA)
pamplemousse grapefruit; various producers
Passoã (P) passion fruit (France)
Pomp & Whimsy Gin Liqueur (P) gin botanicals plus
    raspberry, cucumber, lychee (Los Angeles, California)
ratafia various fruits and/or nuts depending on region
    (primarily Europe)
Southern Comfort (P) secret recipe with various fruits and spices
    (USA)
thibarine (P) possibly dates (secret recipe) (Thibar, Tunisia)
Trauktiné Dainava (P) fruit juices (apple, lingonberry, cherry,
    rowanberry) (Lithuania)
Tuaca (P) brandy-based vanilla bean (fruit of an orchid), citrus
    and spices (Italy)
Zirbenz Stone Pine Liqueur (P) fruit from Arolla stone pine
    (Austria)

Anise Liqueurs

anisette (originally France)
Herbsaint (P) (New Orleans, Louisiana)
mistrà (Marche, Italy)
Salmiakki Koskenkorva vodka base, salmiak liquorice
    (Koskenkorva, Finland)
sambuca (Italy); proprietary brands include Lazzaroni, Luxardo,
    Meletti, Molinari, Ramazzoti
sassolino (Modena, Italy)

French Amers (P)

Amer Picon orange peels, gentian, quinquina
Bonal gentian, quinquina
China-China Valencia and bitter oranges, gentian, quinquina, anise, clove, other Alpine herbs
Dubonnet aromatized wine base with emphasis on quinquina
Salers gentian
Suze gentian

Italian Amari (P)

Amaranca Sicilian wild orange and herbs
Antica Erboristeria Cappelletti Pasubio Vino Amaro alpine liqueur with pine, herbs, wild blueberries
Aperol bitter and sweet oranges, gentian, rhubarb, cinchona and others
Averna bitter orange, pomegranate seeds, sage, liquorice, juniper
Brancamenta Fernet-Branca botanials plus oil of peppermint
Braulio juniper, gentian, wormwood, yarrow, peppermint
Campari secret recipe, but bitter orange is prominent
Cappelletti Sfumato Rabarbato dried Chinese rhubarb
Cardamaro cardoon, calumba, cloves, licorice root, cardamom
Cynar artichokes and other botanicals
Dell'Erborista botanicals and honey
Dell'Etna rhubarb, vanilla, mint, star anise, cinnamon, almond
Di Bormio Alpine style, gentian, rhubarb, mint and others
Fernet-Branca gentian, saffron, rhubarb, camomile and others
Lucano wormwood, gentian, citrus peels and others
Meletti clove, anise, saffron, orange peel, gentian, violet flowers
Montenegro artemisia, coriander seeds, oregano, marjoram, cinnamon, nutmeg, cloves, sweet and bitter oranges
Nardini grappa base, bitter orange, gentian, peppermint
Nerone various herbs, roots, spices
Nonino grappa base, orange, gentian, rhubarb, thyme, wormwood

Ramazzotti Calabrian oranges, rhubarb, gentian, star anise, cinchona

San Simone 39 botanicals including gentian, cinchona, wormwood, rhubarb root, marjoram

Santoni 34 botanicals including rhubarb, iris flower, olive leaf, rose, elderflower

Zucca Rabarbaro Chinese rhubarb, bitter orange peel and others

Kräuterlikör

Becherovka (P) twenty botanicals including cinnamon and cloves (Czechoslovakia)

Jägermeister (P) secret recipe of spices (Germany)

Killepitsch (P) herbs and spices (Germany)

Kuemmerling (P) herbs and spices (Germany)

pelinkovac primarily wormwood (Croatia)

Riga Black Balsam (P) 24 ingredients including withy, gentian and Peruvian balsamic oil (Latvia)

Schwartzhog (P) wormwood, buckbean and other forest botanicals (Germany)

Underberg (P) herbal extracts from 43 countries (Germany)

Zwack Unicum multiple botanicals (Hungary)

Miscellaneous Herbal and Spice Liqueurs

alkermes/alchermes multiple spices often with rose, vanilla, citrus (originally Italy)

allspice or pimento dram allspice in rum base (West Indies)

Amago Obrero (P) herbal (Argentina)

Ancho Reyes, Original and Verde (P) sun-dried chillies (USA)

Apologue Saffron (P) saffron plus coriander, turmeric, nigella seed and other spices (USA)

AROMATIQUE (P) spices (Germany)

Avèze (P) gentian root (France)

Beirão (P) various herbs and seeds, including mint, cardamom and lavender (Portugal)

Bénédictine (P) 27 herbs with angelica, lemon balm and hyssop as main ones (France)

Biancosarti (P) herbs, spices, bark, roots, flowers (Bologna, Italy)

Calisaya (P) Italian-style amaro with cinchona calisaya bark (USA)

Cap Corse Mattei (P) muscatel wine base with quinquina or cinchona (France)

centerba alpine plants (Italy)

Chartreuse (P) secret recipe with 130 herbs (France)

Corfinio (P) herbal with saffron (Italy)

Dolin Génépy (P) artemisia steeped in neutral spirit (France)

Domaine De Canton Ginger (P) eau de vie and cognac base with ginger, honey and vanilla bean (France)

Dunkeld Atholl Brose malt whisky, heather honey, oats and honey (Scotland)

Elisir d'Erbe Barathier (P) multiple botanicals (Italy)

Elixir d'Anvers (P) thirty-plus botanicals, aged in oak (Belgium)

Fireball Whisky (P) Canadian whiskey base with cinnamon flavouring (not to be confused with the malt-based Fireball Cinnamon Whisky)

Galliano (P) more than thirty ingredients, including cinnamon, vanilla, lavender and anise (Italy)

Get 27 (P) mint (France)

herbero multiple herbs plus anise (Spain)

hierbas Ibicencas multiple herbs macerated in anise spirit (Spain)

Izarra (P) yellow and green (peppermint) versions (France)

King's Ginger (P) ginger (England)

Kronan Swedish Punsch (P) spices in a Batavia arrack, Jamaican or Guyanese rum base (Sweden)

Maharan Mahansar Shahi Gulab (P) various herbs, spices and dried fruits (India)

mamajuana rum-based (Dominican Republic)

palo de Mallorca gentian or cinchona (Spain)

Pimm's Cup (P) gin base with various herbs and spices (England) (other proprietary fruit or summer cups include Bloom, Plymouth and Sipsmith)

Punch Fantasia (P) rum with spice and citrus (Italy)

Rumple Minze (P) peppermint (originally Germany, now USA with 'imported flavours')

Schrobbelèr (P) 43 herbs (Netherlands)

Singeverga (P) vanilla and spice (Portugal)

Strega (P) seventy herbs and spices including mint, cinnamon, iris, juniper and saffron (Italy)

Sweetdram Escubac (P) cardamom, nutmeg, caraway, citrus (England)

tentura brandy or rum with spices, especially cinnamon/cloves (Greece)

Verveine du Velay lemon verbena with other herbs, plants and spices (France)

vespetrò medicinal plants, herbs, spices (Lombardy, Italy)

Honey Liqueurs

Amaro Sibilla (P) honey (Pievebovigliana, Italy)

Bärenjäger (P) grain spirit base and honey (Oelde, Germany)

Drambuie (P) Scotch whisky with heather honey and spices (Scotland)

Glayva (P) Scotch whisky with honey, tangerine and spices (Edinburgh, Scotland)

krupnik honey (Poland)

pontche sugar-caned spirit flavoured with molasses or honey (Cape Verde)

rakomelo tsikoudia base spirit with honey and often herbs and spices (Crete)

ronmiel de Canarias rum base with honey (Canary Islands)

Yukon Jack (P) Canadian whiskey base, honey (Salaberry-De-Valleyfield, Canada)

xiboquinha cachaça distillate with honey, lime and spices (Brazil)

Xtabentún rum and honey spirit with anisette added (Yucatan, Mexico)

Liqueurs of Nuts, Seeds, Roots

amaretto various combinations of apricot kernels, peach
  stones and/or almonds (Italy); proprietary examples
  include Disaronno Amaretto Originale, Lazzaroni, Luxardo
Frangelico (P) hazelnuts with coffee, cacao and vanilla (Italy)
kümmel caraway, cumin, fennel (Netherlands, Germany, Russia)
L'Orgeat neutral cane spirit base with almonds (USA)
nocello walnuts or hazelnuts (Modena, Emilia-Romagna, Italy)
nocciolino di Chivasso hazelnuts (Chivasso, Italy)
nocino unripe green walnuts (Emilia-Romagna)
Padre Peppe (P) walnuts (Altamura, Italy)
Sikkim Cardamom Liqueur (P) cardamom (India)

Select Bibliography

Braudel, Fernand, *The Structures of Everyday Life:*
   The Limits of the Possible, vol. I, trans. Siân Reynolds
   (New York, 1981)
Craddock, Harry, with additions by Peter Dorelli, *The Savoy*
   Cocktail Book [1930] (London, 1999)
Dioscorides, *De materia medica*, trans. T. A. Osbaldeston and
   R.P.A. Wood (Johannesburg, 2000)
Dubuisson, *L'Art du Limonadier* (Paris, 1804)
Duplais, Pierre, *A Treatise on the Manufacture and Distillation*
   of Alcoholic Liquors, trans. and ed. M. McKennie
   (London, 1871)
Embury, David A., *The Fine Art of Mixing Drinks*
   (New York, 1948)
Ferguson, Niall, *Civilization: The West and the Rest*
   (New York, 2011)
Gately, Iain, *Drink* (New York, 2008)
Grassi, Elvezio, *1000 Misture* (Bologna, 1936)
Haigh, Ted, *Vintage Spirits and Forgotten Cocktails*
   (Beverly, MA, 2009)
Hewett, Edward, and W. F. Axton, *Convivial Dickens*
   (Athens, OH, 1983)
Mew, James, and John Ashton, *Drinks of the World* (London,
   1892)
Mintz, Sidney W., *Sweetness and Power: The Place of Sugar*
   in Modern History (New York, repr. 1986)
Rorabaugh, W. J., *The Alcoholic Republic* (New York, 1979)

Thenon, Georges Gabriel (known as RIP), *Cocktails de Paris* (Paris, 1929)

Wondrich, David, ed., with Noah Rothbaum, *Oxford Companion to Spirits and Cocktails* (New York, 2021)

Websites and Associations

Difford's Guide
www.diffordsguide.com
Comprehensive website of cocktail recipes,
product information and history

Distilled Spirits Council of the United States
www.distilledspirits.org

EUVS Vintage Cocktail Books
https://euvs-vintage-cocktail-books.cld.bz
Downloadable scans of historical cocktail books
from around the world

Old Spirits Company
www.oldspiritscompany.com
Intriguing selection of vintage liqueurs,
many of them no longer in production

Spirits Review by Chris Carlsson
https://spiritsreview.com
Comprehensive news, reviews, etc.

Taste Atlas
www.tasteatlas.com
Foods and drinks from around the world, all classified by country

Acknowledgements

Any exploration of history is very much like Alice falling down the rabbit hole. It can take a very long time, and it's easy to get distracted by all the bits and baubles along the way. The history of liqueur is filled to the brim with distractions and choosing how to explore the story is very much a personal one. For me, liqueur is a romance that weaves through the centuries, sometimes a full-blown love affair and at other times a simple tryst. The further I explored, the more I uncovered. And I still feel like there are mountains of information to discover. Given the labyrinthine world of liqueur, it comes as no surprise that I got lost in my research and writing many times. Indeed, the story I've told is one that dips its finger into the pies of many other Reaktion books in the Edible series, particularly *Cocktails*, *Spices* and *Sugar*.

Thanks are due to so many people: Jakob S. Bjarnason, Natalie Bovis, Jared Brown, Salvatore Calabrese, Kira Cappello, Alex Ciobanu, Heidi Chen, Tanya Cohn, Albert De Heer, Marcovaldo Dionysos, Peter Dorelli, Megan Eberly, Camper English, Barbara Faini, Simon Ford, Stephen Gould, Steven Grasse, Una Green, Sebastian Hamilton-Mudge, Kaj Hakkinen, Edgar Harden, Miranda Hayman, Jasmine Hawkridge, Heirloom Liqueurs, Robert Hess, Kaarina Jannin, Marc Kerger, Alex Kratena, Landhuis Chobolobo, Victor Lilue, Shuhui Lim, Matteo Luxardo, Keith McIntosh, Stacey Mire, Jeffrey Morgenthaler, Ashley Ott, Daniela Porro, Rachel Harrison Communications, Drew Record, Sam Ross, Matthew Rowley, Aditya Sangwan, Manuela Savona, Tess Sawyer, Eric Seed, Willie Shine, Joshua Steinfeld, Sother Teague, Afton Thompson-Witt,

Kayla Tobey, John Troia, Nathan van der Haegen, Ton Vermeulen, Dave Whitton and Emily Williams. To my discerning publisher, Michael Leaman, you are one of the most forbearing and generous souls I know. To my Edible series editor, Andy Smith, thank you for the original and ongoing opportunity to work with Reaktion. My editor Amy Salter and my picture editor Susannah Jayes were thorough and specific. The most important is saved for last. To my husband, you are my greatest champion, my most honest critic and my North Star. To my son, you amaze me every day with your humour, insight, ingenuity and kindness.

My rabbit hole was much longer than Alice's, but I finally reached Wonderland.

Thank you, sugar, for making it all possible.

Photo Acknowledgements

The author and publishers wish to thank the organizations and individuals listed below for authorizing reproduction of their work.

Courtesy of Haus Alpenz: pp. 33, 86, 109, 110; courtesy of Amarula: p. 134; author's collection: p. 117 (Public Domain); courtesy of Lucas Bols: pp. 40, 89, 135, 140; Brooklyn Museum: p. 36 (Museum Collection Fund/Accession Number 40.16); courtesy of The Canberra Distillery: p. 52 centre; courtesy of the Division of Rare and Manuscript Collections, Cornell University Library: p. 119 (Public Domain); courtesy of Andrew Currie: p. 155; courtesy of Disaronno: p. 147; Flickr: p. 124 (David Zellaby); courtesy of Marcovaldo Dionysos: p. 160 (Credit: Darren Edwards); courtesy of Foss Distillery: p. 156; courtesy of Giffard-Bigallet: pp. 70, 102; courtesy of Golden Moon Distillery: p. 101; courtesy of William Grant & Sons: 13; Hardenberg-Wilthen AG: p. 22; courtesy of Rachel Harrison Communications: p. 159; courtesy of Hayman's Gin: p. 52 right; courtesy of Kahlúa: p. 130; courtesy of Luxardo: p. 88; courtesy of Mast-Jägermeister U.S.: p. 103; courtesy of Nixta: p. 157; courtesy of Old Spirits Company: pp. 10, 64, 121, 137; Drew Record: p. 23; courtesy of Science History Institute: p. 9 (Public Domain); courtesy of Senior & Co: pp. 35, 43, 45; courtesy of Officina Profumo-Farmaceutica di S.M.Novella: pp. 26–7, 56; © Succession Picasso/DACS, London 2023: p. 100; Public Domain: pp. 20, 24, 38, 49, 60, 65, 67, 74, 76, 79, 116; courtesy of Sipsmith London: p. 52 left; courtesy of David Solmonson: p. 133; Lesley Jacobs Solmonson: p. 6; courtesy of Sother Teague: p. 144; courtesy of Tempus Fugit Spirits:

Index

italic numbers refer to illustrations; **bold** to recipes

Apple Pucker 142
  see also DeKuyper
Appletini 142–3
aqua ardens 21, 25, 41
  see also burning water
Arab world 19, 21–3, 25–6, 28,
  30–33, 41, 58
Archard, Franz Karl 73
  see also Andreas Marggraf;
  sugar beets
artificial colours/flavours 132,
  151, 154
aurum potabile 21
Avicenna 25
Aztecs 35–6
  see also cacao

Baileys 35, 128, 132, 133, *133*,
  136–8, 151, 154
Bénédictine *12*, 14, 28, 75, 77,
  113–14, 168
Beta vulgaris altissima, the
  sugar beet *72*
Bigallet & Jinot *102*
Bijou, Ritz version **164–5**
bitterness 34, *86*, 91–2, 98,
  170
bitters, non-potable 93, 114
  see also Angostura bitters
Björk Birch Liqueur *156*
Bols Distillery *40*, 44, 63, 131,
  158
Bonaparte, Napoleon 66–7,
  72–3, 87, 93, *116*
Boomerang 150, **165**
Bradsell, Dick 143, 145, 148,
  168–9

  see also Bramble; Espresso
  Martini
Bramble **168–9**
brandewijn 26, 41
  see also brandy; burned
  wine
brandy 11, 28, 41, 50–51, 59, 78,
  93, 100, 115, 117, 130, 160,
  163, 166
  see also brandewijn; burned
  wine
British East India Company 47
Brizard, Marie 63, *65*, 158
Brunschwig, Hieronymous
  38, 39
Burdock Blood Bitters *116*
burned wine 26
  see also brandewijn
burning water 21, 25, 41
  see also aqua ardens
Bustanoby brothers 120–21,
  129
  see also Café des Beaux
  Arts; Forbidden Fruit

cacao 35, *36*
  see also Aztecs; crème de
  cacao
café culture 13, 57, 59–60, 62,
  66, 68, 83, 94–5, 104
  see also lemonade
Café des Beaux Arts *119*, 120
  see also Forbidden Fruit
Cappiello, Leonetto, 'Marie
  Brizard & Roger'
  advertising poster *65*
cardamom 17, 29–30, 31